GREAT HOUSES OF NEW ENGLAND

Great Houses of New England

New England

TEXT BY RODERIC H. BLACKBURN
PHOTOGRAPHY BY GEOFFREY GROSS

RIZZOLI
NEW YORK

CONTENTS

FOREWORD

GEOFFREY GROSS

In memoriam–

COUSIN DARA JEANNE KAUFMAN *of South Freeport, Maine*
June 20, 1983–June 19, 2006

OPPOSITE *Interior view from Hill-Stead with painting of bather by Edgar Degas (p. 196)*

FOLLOWING PAGES *Scenic view of New England gardens.*

So there I was, driving up the Maine Turnpike, Roxy Music blaring from my shattered minivan sound system, on my way to an early house I had just been told about. On the seat next to me—the initial galley proofs of what was to become the book you are now reading. Almost three years since *Great Houses of New England* was begun I now, for the first time, was able to see the results—organized, edited, and presented in a manner most cohesive.

To find and photograph outstanding examples of architecture representative of this entire region had become a daunting task—and at times seemed utterly impossible. It was never my intent to present the *greatest* houses—this was not to be a contest—but outstanding houses relating to the region, climate, topography, and, most importantly, the people of New England— be they pioneers from other shores or native born. My many travels throughout the New England region—both for this book and the forthcoming *Old Houses of New England* was (and continues to be) indeed a privileged journey.

Through the architecture and decorative arts we see the development of a people and their region—as individuals, through business and commerce, work and leisure, through every facet of their lives as the region evolved and grew, as the country moved to become a new, independent republic, and then onward into a major world leader. Every aspect of this culture and society can be seen and mapped through the study and interpretation of the houses.

The houses that follow have great things to share with us. All houses speak—each and every one has something to say—one need only listen.

INTRODUCTION

Writing a book is like cooking, what you begin with is not what you land up with, partly on purpose, partly by accident. So it has been with this book. The idea for the book was initiated by photographer Geoffrey Gross, just as he had done with our previous book together, *Dutch Colonial Homes in America*, and with his subsequent book with others *Stone Houses: Traditional Homes of Pennsylvania's Buck's County and Brandywine Valley*. Exploring the surviving architectural heritage of New England was a logical next choice. Although the subject had been well covered before by excellent authorities, the visual impact of the houses about which these authors wrote was limited by the photography of their day. Today, through advanced technology and the skill of an exceptional photographer and printer, these houses can be presented in a book with exquisitely true-to-life light and color. With this advantage, and with so much scholarship already published, we have concentrated on revealing images rather than extensive text. Since most readers are new to this knowledge, however, it is appropriate to not only identify the basic history of each houses' community, owner/builder, structure and style, but to give the reader a concise understanding of how New England houses came to be. This introduction aims to serve that purpose.

CONCEPTS

First, some basic concepts should be understood. Houses change over time as new generations of builders and owners take advantage of evolving personal taste and means, architectural knowledge, available materials, and changing social and environmental conditions. All change is based on each owner making decisions as to what is appropriate for needs and means, taking into account how a home must service owner and family—practically, socially, and culturally. It is a complex personal process for which researchers have little access today to all the variables an owner once had to consider in creating a home. The most important exception is the surviving house itself, usually the chief evidence architectural historians have available to "read" its origins, style, and function. Yes, we are grateful for any other evidence that may exist to flesh out an understanding of the owner and his work, such as documents, furnishings and archeological artifacts, but the house itself is the best teacher. Historic buildings are the largest, most complex and expressive artifacts of our historical past. They are the most experiential means we have for learning from our past to better understand who we are and what we may become. The field of historic preservation of our manmade environment may first appeal to our nostalgic curiosity about the past, but it is justified by its ability to help shape our future by allowing us to better realize that past. For that purpose, our historic houses teach us by participation, much as schools, historical novels, television, and movies do.

In order to understand early houses we should not only experience them first hand (or vicariously through media presentation like this book) but learn the tools for describing them: terminology, basic structural and stylistic characteristics and functional uses. Early houses have a structural form composed of timber framing or stone or brick walls. The shape, size, and juxtaposition of these materials reflect a *tradition* of building passed from one generation of owners and builders (housewrights, to use the early term) to the next, each making little or large changes as his circumstances and beliefs allow or dictate. In addition to structure, houses have complementary features such as windows, doors, moldings, chimneys, fireplaces, mantles, which evolved in the same way as the structure. Long evolving structures and their features have a consistency of *style* which includes similarity of surfaces and details such as color, shaping, and materials, which results in a harmonious whole. Thus the house is said to have *integrity*, which aptly reflects the cultural beliefs, aesthetic standards, and functional appropriateness accepted and approved by the community and society that created it. This is what we mean by traditional building; it reflects a continuity with past styles.

Like the accretions houses take on with successive owners resulting in different stylistic features, the vocabulary used to describe them has also evolved, sometimes in confused ways, which persist in the current literature. We should distinguish,

OPPOSITE *A. Everett Austin House*

18

ENGLISH AND AMERICAN ARCHITECTURAL PERIODS AND STYLES

HOUSE OF	MONARCH	REIGN	HISTORIC PERIOD	ENGLISH STYLE	AMERICAN PERIOD INCEPTION DATE	AMERICAN STYLE
Tudor		Elizabeth I	1558–1603	Elizabethan	Tudor Gothic Tudor Renaissance	
						Post-Medieval tradition (First Period, Pilgrim)
Stuart	James I	1603–1613	Jacobean	Tudor Renaissance Stuart Renaissance		
Stuart	Charles I	1613–1649	Carolean	Stuart Renaissance	1620	Puritan
Commonwealth	Oliver Cromwell as Lord Protector	1653–1658	Cromwellian	Cromwellian	1650	Puritan
Commonwealth	Richard Cromwell as Second Lord Protector	1658–1659	Cromwellian	Cromwellian	1650	Puritan
Stuart	Charles II	1661–1685	Restoration	Baroque	1660	Puritan
Stuart	James II	1685–1689	Restoration	Baroque	1685	Puritan Classical tradition (Second Period, Georgian)
Orange	William III	1689–1702	William & Mary	Baroque	1670	Puritan, Baroque
Stuart	William III and Mary	1689–1694	William & Mary	Baroque	1690	Puritan, Baroque
Stuart	Queen Anne	1702–1714	Queen Anne	Baroque	1700	Puritan, Baroque
Hanover	George I	1714–1727	Georgian	Early Georgian Palladian	1715	Puritan, Baroque
Hanover	George II	1727–1760	Georgian	Mid-Georgian	1730	Georgian
Hanover	George III	1760–1820	Georgian	Late Georgian, Regency	1760 1790	Georgian Federal
Hanover	George IV (as Prince Regent)	1811–1820	Regency	Regency	1810	Federal
Hanover	George IV	1820–1830	Regency	Late Regency Greek Revival	1820	Federal/ Greek Revival
Hanover	William IV	1830–1837	William IV	William IV	1830	Greek Revival
Hanover	Victoria	1837–1901	Victorian	Victorian Victorian Early English Victorian Norman Victorian Elizabethan Victorian Gothic	1840 1850 1860 1870 1870 1870 1875 1880 1875 1890	Gothic Revival Italianate French Second Empire Carpenter Gothic Late Gothic High Gothic Stick Style Romanesque Revival Shingle Style Queen Anne Colonial Revival Grand Tour Style
Hanover	Edward VII	1901–1910	Edwardian	Edwardian	1890 1890 1905–30 1910 1930 1920–40 1900–40 1900–20 1925 1930–45	Beaux Arts/ American Renaissance Style Art Nouveau Arts & Crafts Style Individual Eclectic Style International; Style, Modern Revivals of Revivals: Tudor Revival Georgian Revival Colonial Revival French Provincial farmhouse Revival Spanish Colonial Revival (first popular in Scarsdale) Mission Revival Pueblo Revival Dutch Colonial Revival Prairie Art Deco Art Moderne

first of all, between house period and house style. Period means a segment of time. Most periods have taken names from English monarchs who reigned in each period. There is a general but not exact correlation between time periods and architectural styles. Thus Tudor style is associated with houses built during the Tudor period (including Henry VIII and Elizabeth I), Jacobean style with the period of James I's reign, Stuart style with the Stuart kings and queens to 1714 (although this is usually also divided into William and Mary style and Queen Anne style). The greater difficulty comes with the term Georgian style which usually lumps anything built within a sphere of classical influence, that is, from the period of Charles II through much of George III's reign. His son was also a George but the style changed and was named for his period as Prince Regent, hence Regency style. Americans followed these terms for period and style until the Revolution when the terms Federal period and style were used. From then on style terms were used to differentiate all the nineteenth century revival styles. However, we went back to using English monarch names for period and style beginning with Queen Victoria. Her reigning period lasted so long (1837–1901) it encompassed many styles, now, and confusingly lumped together as "Victorian." We would do well to recognize the difference between period and style, using the term "Victorian" only for the period so that we will cease to homogenize a rich period of many divergent styles.

We also speak of *vernacular* and *academic* architecture. Vernacular buildings are those that follow a structural system and style that is indigenous to a region, that is, a tradition passed on for generations, even centuries, by housewrights without the benefit of formal training in the profession of architecture. Houses of New England's Puritan century were almost exclusively built in a vernacular tradition, which had its antecedents centuries before in the towns and farmlands from whence the Puritans came, the southeastern and southwestern counties of England. Careful studies of surviving houses have demonstrated how closely New England houses were patterned after those in the very villages the Puritans came from in England. Since the style of these mostly wooden houses date back to the Medieval period it is appropriate to refer to the New England examples as Post-Medieval. As they had persisted with relatively little change in England, so they did in New England.

POST-MEDIEVAL HOUSES

Houses of the seventeenth century share much in common in terms of post-and-beam construction and decorative features. They were constructed with a rather complex structural system of posts and beams, which, in the fully developed houses, had a central chimney with fireplaces for each room on two floors and a winding stairway just inside the front door. Some were built with a projecting enclosed front "porch" entryway. Most were one room deep but, on many, a lean-to added to the rear created a larger kitchen, the form resembling a box for salt, and hence the common name saltbox for this configuration. Many were built with a second floor, which extended outward a foot or two on one or more sides. The obvious difference from English houses was the New Englanders' use of clapboard siding, a concession to a harsher climate requiring protection of timbers and waddle-and-daub (sticks and mud) in-fill, left exposed in the old country. Throughout the eighteenth century, houses continued to be built in the basic Post-Medieval style but began to change, not so much in structural system but in features. Some houses were made larger, with a different style of window, stairway, door, fireplace, and paneling, yet retained the flavor of the early house. Somewhat arbitrarily, we have decided to treat the Post-Medieval house in another companion book to this one.

The Post-Medieval New England house continued to be built, with some changes, throughout the eighteenth century, especially by families of modest means in more out-of-the-way locations, where similar earlier houses were still the norm. But New England was a land of selective prosperity from the start. Enterprising persons began to exploit natural resources (fish, land, and timber) for personal gain, which encouraged others to facilitate these commodity transactions by setting up saw mills, shipyards, and associated crafts and industries, so that others could provide transport (ships) to facilitate regional and international trade in a wider range of commodities (sugar, rum, slaves) and import (later export, too) manufactured goods, which brought increasing wealth for all who participated. Enterprise coupled with ingenuity by the nineteenth century created a new form of business: mass-production manufacturing, the result of harnessing water power to Industrial Revolution machinery to create textiles, tools, and much more.

Becoming wealthy was for most not an end in itself but a means to the satisfaction of several needs; the need for comfort (a bigger and better house), for social recognition (an advantageous marriage and group of social connections), for political influence (elected and appointed offices), for business expansion (partnerships, contracts), for a secure retirement, for children (enough assets for passive income and inheritance), and personal salvation and satisfaction (supporting charity and the church). The goals in life were, first, finding your way in the world, then making your way in the world, and then insuring your way in posterity.

THE CLASSICAL HOUSE

There was a parallel universe of European building, which had little affect on the rural and town Post-Medieval vernacular tradition, but which would come to dominate public and private building throughout Europe and, later, in the New World. In style, it was classical, derived from the Roman building tradition of the Republic and Empire. That tradition was itself heavily influenced by earlier Greek public buildings, especially temples. While Roman and Greek buildings shared the use of columns, bases, and capitals, the Romans innovated the arch, which allowed them to create more volumetric structures of greater space, light, and variety than Greek building techniques.

With the fall of the Roman Empire that building tradition was nearly terminated. What followed was the Dark Ages, out of which the Medieval style evolved. Not until the sixteenth century did Italians begin to pay attention to ancient classical building, nearly all in ruins. This was the Renaissance, culturally a rediscovery of classical architecture, but dependant upon a society-wide shift in food production, wealth, trade, governmental organization, and knowledge. This was the beginning of the age of academic architecture, based on professional study and the application of standardized principles, proportions, and features derived from classical structures. Italian architects like Alberti, Serlio, Scamozzi, and Palladio not only built villas, churches, and public buildings but they published books on what they did and what they understood the rules of classical architecture to be. They established the cannon of the classical for all time, or so they thought. Their books were disseminated throughout Europe, republished or adapted by later architects, establishing the classical as *the* accepted style for centuries.

Humans by nature, of course, do not follow rules voluntarily and Palladianism, after the most influential of the Italian architects, was at first adopted and then adapted by his followers, first in Italy and then elsewhere. The hard and fast Roman rules the Renaissance builders thought they had discovered in the ancient ruins, kept getting reworked. Truth has to be rediscovered time and again in arts, sciences, and religion. And so it proved to be. Every few generations a new apostle of the "true classical" was born. In England, the architectural Renaissance began in the time of Henry VIII and Elizabeth I with just a few hints of classical columns and arches. It would take a genius to rediscover the whole classical past and create an integrated architecture.

That rediscovery of the wonders and beauty of Roman architecture had already inspired the Grand Tour where artists and aristocrats made their way to Italy to see for themselves what this was all about, in the process also discovering Renaissance paintings, sculpture, landscapes, and gardens. One artist was Englishman Inigo Jones (1572–1652), who came to Italy about 1600, fell in thrall to Palladio's villas, studied the latter's books, and brought the new architecture to England, first in the form of stage scenery for masques and balls (his then occupation), and then, commissioned by King James I, he designed Queen's House at Greenwich in 1618, followed by Banqueting House at Whitehall Palace, London, the next year. Where England had seen elements of the Renaissance before, now it had the New Style, a fully developed set of classical principles which later became the basis of English books on the subject used by ambitious land owners to create their city and country homes. Jones did not publish, but he left hundreds of drawings and his structures were there for inspiration. Other seventeenth-century writers—Italian, French, and English—did publish books on how to build structures, but their

1. *Peter Sergeant House, Boston, 1676–9, conjectural restoration of north gable by R. E. Collins (when the remains of the building were taken down in 1922).* From Thomas T. Waterman, *The Dwellings of Colonial America*, University of North Carolina Press, 1950.

illustrations were minimal and therefore not useful to New England colonial builders in that century. After his death, Jones's influence began to wane, his "true classical" began to go astray in the hands of lesser builders. It would take later geniuses to rediscover Palladianism again and again—first Christopher Wren, later Lord Burlington.

With the Great Fire of London in 1666, the center of the city had to be rebuilt, and Christopher Wren was the architect to do it. His works were also in the classical style but not strictly after the Italian. He incorporated Baroque features like broken and scrolled pediments, rusticated quoins, and rich carving on interiors, which were to prove appealing to New Englanders. He also adopted the wider use of brick, something New Englanders did not much follow as they had scarce access to lime to set bricks. For late seventeenth-century New Englanders, the New Style was unknown and unavailable with the exception of its mental or drawn import to the colonies by arriving officials, especially new governors, who sought to confirm their authority and prestige by building what they had seen in England.

The first inkling of classical style features in New England was a house built by Boston merchant Peter Sergeant in 1676–9 (fig. 1). It dwarfed anything built in New England to that time. It was of two-foot thick brick walls, two-and-a-half stories, with massive end chimneys projecting four feet from the wall that

2. Province House, Boston, as remodeled from the Sergeant House, 1728. From S. A. Drake, Landmarks and Historic Personages of Boston, *1874.*

extended above a coped gable, ending in six diagonally set chimneys for two fireplaces on each floor on each gable end. Such a "roll" gable had first appeared in Elizabethan England in the 1570s along with classical columns, initiating the Tudor Renaissance in architecture which continued through the reign of James I (often, but confusingly, referred to as Jacobean style since more than one style occurred during his period). Bacon's "Castle," c.1655, in Surry County, Virginia, is the only surviving house of this type in America.

Sergeant's house brought him prominence, an example of the importance of a house as promoter of personal status. He became a judge, member of the governor's council, and married the window of a former governor. Even after his death in 1714 the house carried on as he might have wished; it was purchased by the province to serve as residence for royal governors. In doing that, the province in 1728 updated some features of the house, adding a pitch roof, a third story, sash windows, and perhaps the large cupola evident in the nineteenth-century engraving shown here (fig. 2). Province House, as the house was now known, evolved into a Georgian mansion, influenced by an even more remarkable predecessor, the John Foster house.

A decade after Sergeant built his home, Colonel John Foster, recently from Buckinghamshire, set out to build in Boston an equally large house, but in an updated style. While it was of brick, three-stories high, seven-bays wide, five chimneys in the gable ends—en masse similar to Sergeant's—it incorporated new style features: carved-stone trim (four full-height pilasters in the Ionic order), balustraded balconies over the eaves, gable parapets, sash windows, in short, a fully conceived large house in the English Palladian genre (fig. 3). A British officer in 1765, on seeing the house, in a letter sent to London remarked that the house must have been done from a design by Inigo Jones or a successor. He may have been right in that, for Lindsay House in Lincoln Inn Fields, London, has essentially the same features. It was built in 1640, and is attributed to Jones or a successor. When Foster died in 1711 the house was inherited by his nephew Thomas Hutchinson whose son Thomas Jr. was born there the same year. Thomas Hutchinson Jr. became lieutenant and then royal governor, and lived in the house until he departed on the eve of the Revolution. He was the only governor not to reside in Province House for, as he said, he had a better house, a century old, yet still the height of fashion. The Foster mansion stood as a beacon of inspiration until 1836, but it took several decades before others were brave or prosperous enough to adopt its revolutionary design.

Despite Foster's foresight, few houses were built in the New Style before 1715 when useful illustrated books began to come to the New World. These came about as a result of a third infusion of stricter classical principles espoused by Lord Burlington, who had returned to Palladio's books and villas (and Inigo Jones' structures and drawings) to formulate a purer Neo-Palladian than was then popular in England. In 1715 Leoni published a new version of Palladio's books, followed by another version by Isaac Ware (1738). Publications of the designs of Inigo Jones were carried out

3. John Foster House, Boston, c.1688. From American Magazine of Useful Knowledge, *1836.*

by William Kent in 1727, Isaac Ware in 1735, and Vardy in 1744. Colin Campbell issued a great volume of English house engravings as *Vitruvius Britanicus*, tipping his hat to the one Roman whose writings on architecture survived to inform the Renaissance, Vitruvius. James Gibbs, like Palladio, in 1728 came out with a book of his own designs, explicitly recommending it to builders "in remote parts of the Country, where little assistance in design is to be secured." Isaac Ware caught the popularity of this approach in his *Complete Body of Architecture* (1756). All of these were weighty tombs for great country homes. It was actually the lesser architect writers who addressed the needs of colonial builders with books for moderate sized houses. Some, like William Haypenny's *Modern Builder's Assistant* (1747), provided designs that were really usable in America. A virtual library of these how-to books reached American colonies and many houses in the New Style were erected, though usually adapting rather than just copying the English book designs.

THE NEO-CLASSICAL "GEORGIAN"

A consideration of surviving great houses of New England begins with Archibald Macpheadris's large brick home in Portsmouth (p. 36 and below), where we see a relationship to the Foster's house and likely to the Boston town hall of 1712–13 (as first constructed), and certainly to the newly built Massachusetts Hall at Harvard. Macpheadris, however, had the benefit of a newly arrived London builder, John Davis (1675–1738), since professionally trained and experienced architects were not to be had, the old English tradition of gentleman designer learning enough to draw out his own house plan, albeit with the collaboration of an experienced local builder and pattern books, continued well into the eighteenth century in the colonies.

The next step in the development of what can now properly be called Georgian was a house built in Boston in 1737–40 by Thomas Hancock (fig. 4). For such an important house it is a loss

Macpheadris-Warner House

4. The Thomas Hancock House, Boston, 1737–40.
From drawing by J. Davis, engraved by T. Illman, c.1850.

that it was taken down in 1865, due to the vicissitudes of urban renewal. However, from measurements and drawings and a fine 1926 reproduction in Ticonderoga, NY, we can envision its importance for New England architecture. Built of dressed granite blocks set in even ashlar courses and sandstone trim "well cut fitted and polished,"with a gambrel (double-slanted) roof and balustrade, it looked out from the south side of Beacon Hill, which, Hancock boasted, ". . . the Kingdom of England don't afford so Fine a Prospect as I have both of land and water." This prosperous bookseller and stationer spared no expense to incorporate gardens, terraces, hedges, walks, trees, shrubs, and flowers. From his London agents he ordered trees (dwarf, espalier, holly, tulip, and plum), and hand painted wallpaper of "landskips" festooned with all manner of birds, flowers, fruit, and monkeys. Finished in 1740 after three years, Hancock hired noted joiner William Moore to add paneling and trim to the parlor and great chamber as late as 1747 (the next year Moore was adding trim to the Isaac Royall House (p. 44). The stairway alone

Isaac Royall House

5. *Shirley Place, Roxbury, MA, for William Shirley (Royal Governor 1741–56), c.1747. Probably designed by architect Peter Harrison*

(which survives in another house today) set standards for fine houses thereafter. It was the first instance in the colonies to incorporate a double spiral newel post, three different spirally twisted stair balusters on each tread and paneled step ends with scrolled blocks. No doubt there were many other progressive features, which are since shadowed in many later homes we see today.

Another contemporary house to set new standards was that of Royal Governor (1741–56) William Shirley (1694–1771), who started construction of Shirley Place (fig. 5) about 1747. Majestically set back 200 yards from the road, it is up on a high foundation with a double flight of steps. The facade is set with single and double sets of pilasters, the first use of giant pilasters since the Hutchinson house. A steep hipped roof's upper deck is surrounded by a balustrade and, as if a crown for a royal governor, a large and elaborate cupola once topped the house. It was the first house to use grooved boards to simulate rusticated stone (see Jeremiah Lee Mansion p. 56 and below). Such advanced design elements suggest an architect like Peter Harrison of Newport, the first of his profession we know of in New England, who was related to Mrs. Shirley. The house was much altered in the Federal style, especially on the inside, by a new owner in 1819. It survives today, moved to another location.

Jeremiah Lee Mansion

From thence we can turn to other houses that have survived intact, including those illustrated in this volume. The Isaac Royall House in Medford (1733, with alterations to 1750) began much earlier as a brick house that both Isaac Royalls (Sr. And Jr.) expanded with wood cladding, permitting an unusual richness of exterior detail, including elaborate window framing connected by spandrel panels. The walls, like Shirley Place, have rusticated ashlar in wood coursing, set off by contrasting colored corner quoins, modillioned cornice, and a central doorway of pilasters. The backside is almost as elaborate but with different features. The Royall House incorporates the three-story facade first used on the Foster-Hutchinson House and which subsequently became standard for the biggest houses for several decades to come.

The Jeremiah Lee House in Marblehead (1768) shares features of some predecessors, including rusticated ashlar coursing, three story facade, a cupola not unlike Shirley Place, but adds a projecting pavilion of three central bays with a pediment at the roof level. Over the front door is a protecting portico with Ionic columns, the precursor of many that appear on later Federal houses. This house is often called the Lee Mansion in homage to its unusual size, seven bays wide, allowing for a stunningly large central hall, more a room than passage.

Outside of the coastal towns of greatest prosperity, Georgian houses continued to be built for a longer period and with less innovation, an understandable consequence of conservative taste and means, a tendency which is neigh-on universal in architectural history. The 1785 Hamilton House (p. 66) is just such a country house. Situated at South Berwick, far upriver from Portsmouth, New Hampshire, it reflects a Georgian plan and features of a generation before, at a time when post-revolutionary Federal design was being introduced into the design centers of the new states.

FEDERAL

What we call Federal architecture, appropriately named for the federal system of government our new nation adopted, has more complex influences to account for its transition from Georgian than the popular notion that it was cultural reaction against our prior political and cultural domination by the English. Indeed most features of Federal houses find counterparts in Georgian ones; it was not a revolution but an evolution. Federal features do appear lighter in mass, thinner in section. But the plan is similar—central hall with square or rectangular rooms on either side. Elevations and fenestration of windows and doors are similar—less bold in detail for sure. The familiar three-story facade of five bays wide was carried over seamlessly to the Federal. That, however, is where the similarity ends and new influences begin.

The Revolution converted Americans from a century of francophobes (remember we and our allies and masters, the British, had fought four French and Indian wars against French Canada) to

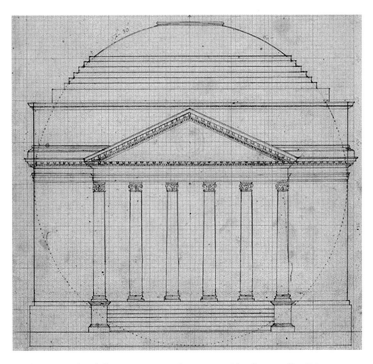

6. The Rotunda of the University of Virginia, Charlottesville, VA, 1823–25. Thomas Jefferson, architect. Designed to convey the "authority of nature and power of reason."

embracing France as a newfound ally when Louis XIV's support tipped our imminent defeat in the Revolution to a hair's-breadth victory. In a complex irony, King Louis lost his head to French Revolutionaries inspired by the very revolution he had supported. To compound irony, the French Revolution, having had no precedent for democracy in royal France, sank into the Terror just when our founding fathers acknowledged their debt for good government to the French Enlightenment. What goes around, comes around.

French intellectuals, including a number of talented architects, fled the Terror in time to save their souls and serve American architecture and city planning. Their ideas brought professionalism and monumentality to public buildings and spaces (especially in Washington D.C.) and certain innovations in domestic houses (French windows and doors, innovative room plans—the octagon and oval—and new types of functional rooms).

Thomas Jefferson played a considerable role in Neo-Classical architecture after the Revolution. A self-made architect, he had traveled widely in Europe, especially in France and Italy, absorbing Roman architecture and the Renaissance villas of Palladio and his contemporaries (Monticello's dome was inspired by his visit to Scamozzi's Villa La Rocca Pisana). Like others before him, he was not satisfied that the true qualities of Roman design were being recognized and built. He introduced his own, more correct, version, first with the Richmond Virginia Capitol (1780), then with his *magnum opus*, the University of Virginia rotunda and pavilions (1817–18) (fig. 6). That rotunda was modeled on the

General George Cowles House

Another influence on Federal architecture was literally dug up. From the 1730s, archeologists were at work excavating long-lost Roman Herculaneum and Pompeii; others were carefully recording Roman and Greek ruins with an eye to rediscovering, yet again, more accurate truths about ancient architecture. Primarily through publications of these discoveries the first fundamental change in Renaissance established doctrine about ancient architecture came about. Since Palladio, it was assumed, and therefore accepted, that there were certain infallible rules of classical architecture. The new discoveries proved otherwise. The classical orders in ancient times varied from building to building, place to place. This upset the Renaissance-established order, supplanting it with almost endless variations on the "truth." Scientific archeology was liberating cultural thought just when Enlightenment thought was liberating political doctrine. The last quarter of the eighteenth century was an exciting time for revolutionaries and intellectuals. In a sense it not only ushered in changes resulting in Federal/Regency architecture, but opened up the possibilities of other revivals. The nineteenth century's succession of architectural styles owes its impetus to these rediscoveries of the past.

The influence of archeology on America came from England when architects like Robert Adams published ancient discoveries such as in *Ruins of the Palace of the Emperor Diocletian at Spaleto on the Dalmatian Coast* (1764). Like Inigo Jones before, Adams (and others) instigated a more exact rediscovery of ancient architecture and decoration, which soon appeared in their books and then in the buildings they created. Thus Georgian became Regency and Federal.

Pattern books were also home-grown in America. Massachusetts builder Asher Benjamin produced a series of books and editions starting with *The County Builder's Assistant* (1796) and *American Builder's Companion* (1806), which gave sufficient illustrated details and instructions to achieve the intent of the titles in smaller towns and on farm. The latter codified Bulfinch's innovations while freely modifying Robert Adams's designs, spreading them widely.

The sum of these influences resulted in what we call Federal style (the English parallel style is Regency), with columns of slender proportions, elliptical fanlights over narrow sidelights for doorways and central windows, spiral stairways, slender, low relief but more detailed decorative moldings—in sum, a refined grace and subtle unity of parts and the whole, the achievement of a sophisticated group of professional architects and their influence through examples and books on a nation of housewrights.

But that was not the end of it. By documenting the diversity of ancient classicism in architecture and thereby exploding the centuries-old "rules" of design, archeology and architects left architecture without an established doctrine, anything was up for challenge and trial. For the next century, try they did, as new waves of revivals seemingly stumbled over each other for acceptance. Ultimately

last Roman building surviving intact, the Pantheon in Rome. A pedimented portico of columns set before a domed main block (in this case round), thanks to Jefferson, became the most popular America ideal for pubic buildings, especially the national and many state capitols and countless court houses across the land. Jefferson's home, Monticello, in its final and present configuration is a paean to Roman and Renaissance principles.

Jefferson undertook a small number of house commissions for family and friends. These are still not well known yet should be, as they bear the design stamp of a superior mind that understood the needs of domestic life and was able to configure them in plan and function within his brand of the Neo-Classical. Without writing about them, his domestic houses by and large remained local. Only occasionally do we see a Federal house in the north in this Roman Revival manner, the George Cowles House in Farmington, Connecticut, being perhaps the finest example (p. 90 and above) in New England. The term Roman Revival is not used in the architectural historical literature because almost all variations of Neo-Classical buildings up to the nineteenth century were really of Roman inspiration. However, in America, Jefferson's designs come far closer to real Roman principles of design than they were all rejected and, in the twentieth century, bypassed by an entirely different conception of the built environment, the Modern. But in the meantime the classical tradition did not expire with Federalism. The classicism of Greece had yet to be explored in architecture as it had already been discovered in archeology.

GREEK REVIVAL

The first of these revivals came out of archeological examination of Greek ruins during the last half of the eighteenth century. The style gained popularity, especially in the United States, in part because it happened to coincide with the beginning, in 1821, of Greek revolt against Turkish Ottoman domination. It was also appealing because of its association with a sense of political and cultural perfection: the birth of democracy in ancient Athens and the perfection of its architecture. Little temples sprang up all over eastern America between the 1820s and 1850s. Simplified versions without columned porticos made useful if small farmhouses. The full-scale temple form, usually adapted or copied from the Parthenon, conveyed a sense of solidity especially appealing to institutions. The first Greek Revival public building was Benjamin Latrobe's Bank of Philadelphia (1799-1801) (fig. 7), using the Greek order of the Erechtheum on the Acropolis at Athens. The first domestic-scale buildings in the Greek style were some of Jefferson's pavilions for the University of Virginia (1817–1818). These were on a scale easily adopted for houses.

Of course apostles of this style were soon to print pattern books as guides to any competent housewright, no matter where

7. The Bank of Philadelphia, Philadelphia, 1799–1801. Benjamin Henry Latrobe, architect. William Birch engraving of 1800 (mistitled "Bank of Pennsylvania").

they lived. Asher Benjamin's *The Practical House Carpenter* (1830) provided "Grecian Orders of Architecture . . . fashioned according to the Style and practice of the Present Day." This was followed closely by Myndart Lafever's *Modern Builder's Guide* (1833) and numerous other books. Curiously, for a style apparently restricted to heavy columns and the lack of the arch, it was adapted to all kinds of buildings: institutional, domestic, commercial, and ecclesiastical; factories and barns excepted. It was also exceptional because it was the first foreign (non-English) architecture in America, virtually dropped into the landscape out of popular enthusiasm starting about 1825 and lasting in some places into the 1850s. It was the first of several European revival styles that brought entirely new designs to America. Some would argue that they were alien to our townscapes and landscapes, lacking indigenous familiarity or natural affinity to America that presaged a late nineteenth-century reaction against that which did not grow out of our environment.

GOTHIC

Much nineteenth-century architecture was a reactionary tussle between the age-old opposition of medieval and classical. A sure bet against the rage for Greek classicism was a Gothic reaction. Gothic is the academic version of medieval vernacular; it was first applied to great souring piles of verticality, Gothic cathedrals. These predated the Renaissance yet resurface persistently, even today (in New York City, the Cathedral of St. John the Devine is still under construction). When it comes to communicating with God, an architecture that imitates the natural grace and towering splendor of great trees is not to be supplanted for long.

The opposition of medieval and classical aesthetics has its motivational counterpart in the human need to express emotion yet sustain intellectual order within the person and, by extension, the society. A look at any style of western architecture, even Modernism, bears this analysis out. In literature and the graphic arts the opposition is usually expressed as Romanticism versus classical "rule of reason."

The rebirth (literally: renaissance) of the Gothic is generally ascribed to Horace Walpole's creation of his country villa, Strawberry Hill near London, in 1751. He did not mean it as a challenge to the all-prevailing classical ("it was but to please my own taste"), however, such a new conception caught on with his weekend guests, refreshed by an outward and visible expression of latent feelings already primed by Romantic literature. A movement sprang up in the guise of a nostalgic idealization of the past. It fixated on the medieval, a mysterious era evoked by vine-covered Gothic ruins (much the product of King Henry VIII's dissolution of the Catholic monasteries after his break with the Vatican). Associations with a chivalrous past of knights and damsels, battlemented castles, and tragic and triumphal events primed a literary public for a return to the Gothic in mortared

Justin S. Morrill Homestead

stock, CT, and the Justin S. Morrill Homestead (1848) in Strafford, VT (p. 152). Like most Gothic structures, they are not copies of the past but highly stylized adaptations designed to evoke an emotional response and thereby confirming to receptive minds the rightness of that half of human nature's yearning for sentiment, serenity, and inner security. The movement was initially a phenomenon of the 1840s but persisted in several named permutations through the rest of the century as High Victorian Gothic, Late Gothic, Stick Style (an unfortunate modern appellation), Queen Anne (nothing to do with her but much to do with promoting the style) and Tudor. Shingle Style and Arts and Crafts owe their inheritance to this vernacular tradition with its age-old emphasis on structure honestly expressed, surfaces *au natural*. Even Richardson Romanesque and Frank Lloyd Wright's Prairie Style owe homage to the principles behind the Gothic Revival.

ITALIANATE

With the exception of the Greek Revival, up until the 1850s the acceptance of new architecture came filtered through well developed English styles. The Greek Revival was transmitted to America through books, its constructed use largely ignored by the English. So too the Italianate, our first real design foray into the continent. The Italianate is loosely derived from medieval Italy, indeed the most obvious feature common to the two are square towers reminiscent of fortified hill towns in which competing Montague and Capulet clans sought to literally overlook each other by building to absurd heights. One is hard pressed to find early houses in Italy that otherwise would suggest what we built here under the label of Italianate. Regardless of its imputed origin, for over a decade Italianate houses were built in great numbers in cities, towns, and on farms. Its use of sizable cornice brackets created a sufficiently prominent "crown" on the face/facade that the mass of a cap-like roof was visually unnecessary. That, combined with new roofing materials, allowed flatter roofs which made it possible to break out of the box/rectangle form, creating projecting rooms, thus new room arrangements and more windows for better light. It was an appealing development, both for its new form and for new functional possibilities. In cities it was revolutionary. With a bold cornice and brackets, a house could be attractively built even though shoulder-to-shoulder with several others. Many could be squeezed into a block, all the rainwater exiting to the rear on a single pitch roof instead of flooding sides or the sidewalk. Countless post-Civil War towns and cities are almost defined by this kind of house. Free-standing Italianate homes, however, far more effectively display the wide possibilities of this form. One of the really great Italianate houses in America (Victoria Mansion, p. 164) was built in far off Portland, Maine, by a pre-air conditioning refugee, hotelier Ruggles Morse, from steamy New Orleans seeking summer relief; it was the dawn of a new age of elegant summer "cottages"

stone. Soon imitations of an imaged past were cropping up all over the English landscape, a landscape already being transfigured from formal rectilineal gardens to sweeping naturalistic vistas by Lawrence "Capability" Brown. His revolution in landscaping was not intended, any more than Walpole had intended, to presage a Romantic movement in architecture, but it did.

In New England, the way for the Gothic was being well prepared by a couple of New Yorkers, architect Alexander Jackson Davis (1803–1892) and landscaper and architectural designer Andrew Jackson Downing (1815–1852). Davis's works and Downing's publications in many editions spread Gothic and Italianate houses, and gardens and landscapes across several states, wrapped in a thoroughly Romantic conception. New Englanders sporadically accepted this return to their post-medieval past. Notable examples are Bowen House (Roseland Cottage, 1848) in Wood-that would run as far as the Depression.

If you take an Italiante house—brackets, towers, and all—and place a high French Mansard roof atop it, you have an American version of a French "Second Empire" house. When Napoleon III reestablished the Empire in 1852 Paris underwent an architectural revitalization. Since buildings were taxed by the number of floors under the cornice, an expanded attic allowed for an untaxed floor (sometimes two). Francois Mansard's (1598–1666) seventeenth-century high-roof style was revived in France, then England and the United States, where the first such building was built (1859–1861) for William Wilson Corcoran by James Renwick Jr. (and now known as the Renwick Gallery in Washington D.C.). For residences, allowing a third floor for servants' rooms without making the house look institutionally too high was appealing. It was an aesthetic accommodation to a functional need brought on by Industrial wealth and a host of willing immigrants seeking domestic employment.

LATE GOTHIC TO QUEEN ANNE

By the late nineteenth century the cycle of fashion sped up, in part because of the mechanization of building parts, which made so much more available. Shops with belt-driven machinery turned out all manner of wood decoration; publications promoted their application in new types of houses. Industrial barons set the pace of taste with extravagant stone and brick mansions and the middle class was ready to ape them in wood.

At this time a set of interrelated styles became popular throughout the country, all inspired by a return to the medieval Gothic, indeed these interrelated styles of 1870–1910 are a logical continuation of that first Gothic Revival of the 1840s, just more elaborate in detail, usually larger and often architect-designed public buildings. But like any style, there were different levels of size, sophistication, and financial investment. Simpler, small, wooden Gothic cottages are what we expect and find in villages, while in cities large elaborate masonry churches and public buildings were constructed, all working off the same inspiration.

Even within these levels were stylistic variations designated by different names: Stick Style, Eastlake, Queen Anne, Tudor, High Gothic, and more. Confusion of categories became more evident as builders and architects borrowed elements from various sources (European, American, their own imagination). Thus a Queen Anne house may have vaguely classical columns. A Stick Style house (which, by the way, isn't made of sticks per se) is decorated with multiples of moldings, turnings, decorative boards, chamfered posts, and much more, usually picked out in contrasting colors. Stick Style also shares features of other styles like the earlier Gothic Revival, Queen Anne, and Tudor Revival. Nevertheless each of these has an internally consistent set of structural and stylistic principles, which makes them appear right for their time and for their style despite borrowings and individualistic invention.

SHINGLE STYLE

The Shingle Style house grew out of New England's coast and weather, with stylistic elements borrowed from Queen Anne (porches, asymmetrical form), Colonial Revival (gambrel roof, lean-to additions, classical columns, Palladian windows), and Richardson's Romanesque (irregular shapes, arches, and use of stone). Shingle siding is still preferred on the coast as it withstands the salt sea air well. The style was favored by wealthy summer residents, who usually built large free-form "cottages" to take in views and air. For the same reasons, interiors were meandering, spacious and vacation comfortable. Uniquely American, architects H.H. Richardson, William Ralph Emerson, John Calvin Stevens and the firm of Mead, McKim & White, were especially active designing in this style, mostly from 1880 to1900. Gustave Stickley borrowed ideas for his American version of the Arts and Crafts Movement, as did Frank Lloyd Wright.

ROMANESQUE REVIVAL

This movement in architecture is so closely bound to its originator, Henry Hobson Richardson (1838–1886), that it is usually referred to as Richardsonian Romanesque. He was briefly a student at the Paris Ecole des Beaux Arts and must have viewed southern European eleventh- and twelfth-century Romanesque buildings. Back in Boston his architectural practice made use of his version of this style: heavy massing of rusticated brownstone in earthy tones, broad round-headed arches supported by squat columns, broad roof gables, conical-topped towers, and exquisite attention to Romanesque-style stone carving. He concentrated on public buildings but he did a few residences (including Stonehurst, p. 176). He influenced other architects, some of whom, like Charles McKim and Stanford White (founders of McKim, Mead & White, New York), had been apprentices in Richardson's office. The style spread to the Mid-West where Louis Sullivan made use of it in his revolutionary steel-frame buildings and later Frank Lloyd Wright's designs reflect its influence. Like most revival styles, its popularity lasted about a generation.

COLONIAL REVIVAL

Like the Shingle Style, the Colonial Revival by its nature was wholly indigenous. By the 1880s America was ready for a change, a century of foreign eclectic revivals had run its fashionable course—fashion may be the butt of perennial jokes but it does serve to refresh the body social, rescuing each generation from its own excessive enthusiasms. The Centennial celebrations of 1876 refocused a nation on its own greatest achievement, creating itself as a body politic. Pride seeks expression, in this case in art and architecture. Builders and architects had quite a grab bag to

Rosecliff

pull ideas out of: thousands of surviving "colonial" homes. Most appealing were Georgian- and Federal-style features which were artfully reassembled into white-painted suburban homes. Fan-light, side-light, and Palladian windows, paneled walls and doors, bold dentilled cornices, McIntire-inspired mantles, sweeping balustered stairways in central halls, louvered-shuttered sash windows; mill shops could produce anything and advertised it. The shop-by-catalog era had begun, for whole houses or any parts. In the hands of architects a balanced ensemble was possible; with owner and contractor access, a new form of eclecticism would prevail, and still does. One of the most impressive, if atypically sprawling, Colonial Revival houses is Hill-Stead (p. 196) near Farmington, Connecticut, built by a talented self-trained architect, Theodate Pope (later Riddle), for parents drawn back to New England by a nostalgic urge to be reunited with their past, friends, and family.

GRAND TOUR REVIVAL

The Grand Tour dates to the early seventeenth century when, initially, the affluent dilatants, diplomats, artists, and architects began this pilgrimage to Rome. By the latter half of the

nineteenth century the Grand Tour was a *de rigeur* initiation into the finer things of life for daughters and sons of the old and newly affluent. Culture, with a capital "C," had always been that which came from Europe. It was imported in droves, Old Master paintings and drawings for the rich, Old Master copies for the county *neuvou riche*. To better demonstrate one's taste to the world beyond the forbidding gates, talented architects were employed to build European style villas and palazzo. New Yorkers were especially bitten by this competition, each trying to out-do, in expense if not taste, neighboring industrialists along Fifth Avenue. When Newport, Rhode Island, became one of their chosen summer resorts, the same build-athon continued, one bigger than the next, yet coyly referred to as "our summer cottage," no matter how grand. Grant Tour Revival eschewed the modesty of the Shingle Style—so naturally adapted to the landscape and shore—in favor of mini-palaces plucked out of England and France. Newport's Rosecliff (p. 212) is a shiny white version of Louis XIV's Grand Trianon near Versailles. The Mount (p. 222), in the Massachusetts Berkshire Hills, was inspired by the Brownlow family's Palladian Belton House (1684–6) in Lincolnshire.

Most architectural styles come to an end because of exhausted fashion; Grand Tour Revival stopped for lack of money, squandered on excess, depleted by income tax, split by egalitarian inheritance, and the Depression. Those white elephants that were not torn down were mostly saved by institutional use, especially museums celebrating the pleasures and follies of excess.

INDIVIDUAL ECLECTICISM

If Grand Tourers lived to build, eccentrics and individualists build to live in their own special way. Relatively unconstrained by the European aristocratic dogma of accepted taste, American individualists could pick and chose from multiple pasts to suit their fancy as they created the perfect house—for themselves. Henry Davis Sleeper (1878–1934) created for himself what turned out to be an immensely popular site, Beauport, at Gloucester (p. 234). An artful pastiche of architectural elements ransacked from New England's past combined with Sleeper's colorful placement of antique furnishings, resulted in a personalized museum setting to beguile his decorator clients.

A. Everett "Chick" Austin Jr. (1900–1957) created an equally personalized version of the past in Hartford (p. 252). An Americanized facade inspired by a Renaissance villa, he filled the inside with his preferences in art and design: European Baroque and Internationalist Modern; the two discretely separated on different floors. The house was as much a family residence as a semi-public setting for entertaining an odd assortment of cutting-edge aesthetes and timidly tantalized latter-day Puritans.

PICKING UP THE PIECES: A CENTURY OF PRESERVATION

Picking which Great Houses in New England should be included in this book has been an interesting task. There are far more such houses to choose from than can be included; the choice was quickly narrowed by a number of criteria: a desire to include houses from each state in New England and from all periods and styles, owners who were willing to be included, houses accessible for photography on a tight schedule, well-preserved early or original features and furnishings, in presentable condition, telling an interesting story of style, history, design, or personalities, and those on which sufficient documentation was available on the history of the house and ownership. Taking these into account reduced the number to the anticipated size of this book. We landed up with nineteen houses that we believe express the finest qualities of New England's domestic building heritage in the long classical tradition. We leave for the next book the many post-medieval early houses and their Georgian successors that dot the villages and farms of New England.

The very fact that there are so many fine houses to choose from is a testament to New England's historic culture. The good sense to design and build fine houses has been matched by a per-

sistent desire by New Englanders to preserve them in numbers greater than in other regions. Yes, many have been lost to neglect, fire, modern urban renewal, periodic rural farm poverty, the urge to modernize, and the sprawl of commercialism. But community pride, even if not matched by community wealth, has helped preserved countless houses (and other building types) for reuse as homes or as house museums. What started as colonial pride after the Centennial became a concerted movement in the early twentieth century. If one person stands out as the spearhead it was William Sumner Appleton (1874–1947). Incensed to passion against the loss of historic houses, he founded the Society for the Preservation of New England Antiquities (SPNEA, now Historic New England) in 1910. Without preservation laws, and with communities limited to saving a favorite building or two, Appleton realized that a regional approach to buying up threatened structures was necessary. The goals extended to preserving them based on careful documentation and research (a high standard Appleton insisted on and which has influenced preservation throughout the country ever since), furnishing at least some to give public understanding of New England's early life and values, and returning others to private ownership with protective covenants. Today, Historic New England owns 125 structures on 45 sites (many others it has stewardship over) and has the most comprehensive collection of New England antiquities anywhere. This book would not appear as it does without Historic New England's leadership and the countless other community and governmental organizations and private owners who have toiled to save their past.

RIGHT *A. Everitt Austin House*

FOLLOWING PAGES *Hamilton House*

MACPHEADRIS-WARNER HOUSE

Portsmouth, NH, 1716–18

At the mouth of the Piscataqua River as it opened onto the Atlantic, just south of present day Portsmouth, one Martin Pring arrived from England in 1603 exploring for opportunity. Just three years after the Pilgrim landfall at Plymouth (1620), a settler would arrive at this advantageous position to find a hub of industry divided between interior and ocean-based resources, especially timber and fish, and a port that remained open throughout the year. The resulting coastal and international trade fostered here a third industry, shipbuilding. Based on renewable resources, the economy of what would become Portsmouth experienced long-term growth. The town became the province's capital in 1679.

The American Revolution ushered in an era of uncertainty. British sea power threatened ports, prompting the new state of New Hampshire to move its capital inland to Exeter. Wartime privateering (state-sanctioned raiding of enemy commerce) swelled captains' coffers in the Revolution and the War of 1812. That wealth circulated to local craftsmen who built handsome Georgian

We know uncommonly more about this early house than most others thanks to the 1990 discovery of its designer/builder's manuscript memorandum book of 1707–1722. John Drew (1675–1738) was an experienced house and ship joiner who arrived at Boston from London in 1710 in time to help build more fireproof brick homes after that post-medieval town's 1711 fire. Scottish seafaring merchant Archibald Macpheadris had arrived there from North Ireland two years before and the two collaborated in building Macpheadris' new home in Portsmouth beginning in 1716. In form, material, and detail, it resembled houses Drew had been building near London not long before. With some alterations and additions (covering the double roof to make one) it remains essentially the same house as built.

PRECEDING PAGES *Ancestral Warner portraits gaze upon the parlor furnished with descendants' possessions. An early alteration lowered the unusually high fireplace opening to one more efficient, the space filled with extra Dutch Delft tiles. Back-to-back corner fireplaces were a rarity then and thereafter although they allowed economical use of a single chimney.*

OPPOSITE *Jonathan Warner purchased this secretary bookcase, attributed to Portsmouth cabinetmaker Robert Harrold (working 1765–1792), about 1765 and installed it in the front sitting room, at the same time concealing under new fashioned wallpaper the original paneling, later discovered to have originally been given Baroque-style freehand painted decoration, now restored.*

RIGHT *Some craft objects achieve elevation to art through the inspired taste and exuberant creativity of a gifted maker. This maple and walnut high chest is attributed to a Portsmouth cabinetmaker, yet unnamed, but inlayed initials, "I+S," identify its first owner as John Sherburne and the date, "1733," is thought to commemorate his marriage to Eleanor Mendam. It first entered the Warner house with Elizabeth Warner Sherburne who moved here to nurse her ailing uncle Jonathan before his death in 1814 (she subsequently inherited the house). It stands as the earliest American Queen Anne–style piece of furniture with an affixed date.*

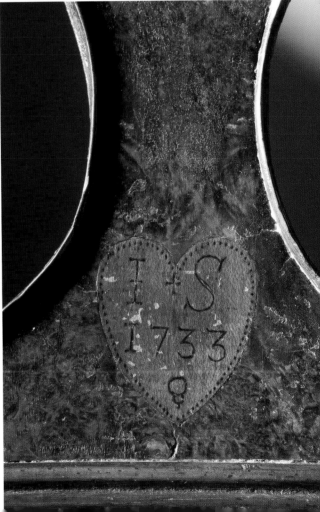

and Federal houses. The new century had a rocky start, however, with extensive fires and severely curtailed trade with other nations caused by the 1807 Embargo Act. Portsmouth recovered somewhat but its sway over New Hampshire affairs diminished. These circumstances turned out to be a blessing for Portsmouth's historic legacy, as much of the old district has been remarkably preserved.

In the early eighteenth century, one of the many whose ingenuity benefited self and community was a Scottish immigrant from northern Ireland, Captain Archibald Macpheadris (c.1680–1729). A merchant and ship owner, he exported timber and naval stores, and also engaged in "the devious trade," importing many luxuries untaxed by his friends in the custom house. He was also a member of Lt. Governor John Wentworth's Royal Council, and married Wentworth's daughter, Sarah. In 1715, Macpheadris bought two lots in a newly subdivided part of town and built an impressive brick Georgian house for his new bride. For the service of designing and supervising construction he hired a newly arrived London-trained builder named John Drew (1675–1738), whose recently discovered memorandum book (1707–1722) details much of the work done for Macphedris.

In Portsmouth, most houses were of clapboard, but Macpheadris and John Drew, took as their model the contemporary styled London merchant's house, which both would have known well. Drew's bill of 1717 totaled £1040.12.4, a large figure at that time. Like its London counterparts, it is rich in interior details,

Striking and unusual are early wall murals in the stairway, some based on print sources, depicting Abraham sacrificing Isaac, a servant spinning flax while looking at a dog barking at an eagle carrying off a chicken. Two Native Americans, one Mahigan (left), the other Mohawk, were copied from mezzotints made of four New York American Indians brought through Boston to Queen Anne's Court in 1710 to persuade her to fund an invasion of New France (Canada) to rid the English colonies of this competitor for furs and land. The Indians were a popular hit in London; the Queen funded the invasion but it failed (her fleet lost its way in the fog of the St. Lawrence River and withdrew), so it took more French and Indian Wars, finally accomplishing the deed in 1760. The mural subjects are more akin to the sensibilities of New York Dutch than a New Englander, but both shared the need to remove the French and Indians from their inland territory. The painter of the murals may have been Nehemiah Partridge, a Portsmouth-born artist who may have trained under John Smibert in Boston and spent most of his career in the Hudson River Valley doing portraits of the Dutch, which would explain the New York echoes.

and has a center hall, four main rooms to the two main floors, a full basement, and an attic story with dormers. Today, it is considered the earliest and finest surviving urban brick mansion in New England. Others were erected earlier in Boston, but none remain.

Drew provided a shingled M-shaped roof, used successfully in the milder English climate. It proved leaky in Portsmouth's icy, snowy winters, and was soon covered with a gambrel, though the center V of the M roof remains inside. The cupola, part of the original scheme, still juts out from the roof to give a commanding view of the harbor. The first kitchen was attached to the west side of the house, but was removed around 1820, when a new summer kitchen was built off the north end.

The interior is laid out with an eye for style as well as function. Entering the hall, the smaller entertaining room is to the left, with the large winter kitchen, scullery, and service spaces behind. To the right of the hall is a large parlor and smaller chamber behind. The back-to-back corner fireplaces in the right rooms (seen elsewhere in Swedish houses near the Delaware River) allow space for two east-facing windows, adding much needed light to the large interior spaces. The rooms on the right have the fireplaces in the standard position, centered on the west wall.

Macpheadris lived only a few years in the house before he died in 1729, leaving it to his wife, Sarah. It was, in turn, inherited by their daughter, Mary, who in 1760 married Jonathan Warner (1726–1814). He outlived both wife and children, bequeathing the house to collateral heirs, the Sherburnes. The house was used in summers only from the 1880s on by Sherburnes and Penhallows until 1930, when it was purchased by the new Warner House Association as a house museum. Many of the furnishings are family objects that have been returned to their place of origin.

ISAAC ROYALL HOUSE

Medford, MA, 1733, 1747–50

LEFT *The west facade, modified by Isaac Royall Jr. after 1739, features full-height corner pilasters and window pediments.*

OPPOSITE *The doorway of the east facade (1732–37) includes pilasters in the Doric order set upon pedestals, perhaps the latter served as inspiration for the novel setting of each window upon a pedestal, joining the windows vertically with panels from base to cornice.*

The progenitor of the Royall family in New England, William, arrived at Salem in 1629, a servant indentured to the Massachusetts Bay Colony Company. Two generations later, his grandson Isaac had moved to Antigua, where he owned numerous slaves, and had accumulated great wealth from his successful sugar plantation.

In 1732 he decided to retire back to the Colonies with his family and purchased 500-odd acres of land and a seventeenth-century farmhouse from John Usher. He then built the brick portion of slave quarters. The clapboard section was added sometime in the 1750s.

The Usher House was two-stories high with ballast brick ends, but just one room deep. Isaac set about transforming it to his own taste. The house was more than doubled in size to a full two-room depth and enlarged to three floors. Both brick-gable ends were widened to accommodate an additional chimney and brick parapets built up between them. The east facade was encased in

clapboards with a profusion of carved wood decoration: angled quoins, richly molded window surrounds connected by spandrel panels, a modillioned (with horizontal brackets) cornice, and a central door with pilasters.

Alas, Isaac Royall Sr. enjoyed his transfigured estate for only two years. At his death in 1739, his son, Isaac Royall Jr. (1719–81) inherited the entire property and modified the west facade considerably. The new facade resembled the front in basic form, but with different details: corner pilasters, pediments over all windows, and an elaborate door surround. Oddly, one gable end was sheathed in clapboards while the other is brick.

With such a drastic enlargement, interior spaces were either rebuilt or redecorated. Royall Jr. spared little expense to bring the house up to a new standard set by the recently constructed Thomas Hancock stone house in Boston (1737–40) by nearly duplicating Thomas Hancock's stairway and two principal rooms, likely using the same craftsman, William More.

OPPOSITE *The double spiral newel post, triple-variant balusters on each step, and the paneled and scrolled step ends are a tour-de-force of a colonial carver's capabilities, perhaps executed by William More, who had created nearly identical features for Thomas Hancock's Boston home (see fig. 4, page 25).*

RIGHT *More symbolic than functional, many large Georgian houses had hallways "divided" by an open archway. An impressive feature in the most public space in the house, it often acted as a subtle divider of public from private space: the rear for private family quarters, the front for public reception.*

LEFT AND OPPOSITE *The best room is full-height paneled throughout, punctuated by window-seated alcoves framed by elliptical arches. The numerous Doric pilasters mimic the east facade door. In later Georgian houses such rich woodwork was omitted in favor of newly available wallpaper. The portrait of Isaac Royall Jr. is derived from the Feke painting of 1741, now at the Harvard Law School. Although this room has a higher ceiling than others, the proportions of the original farmhouse around which the larger structure was wrapped dictated lower ceilings than those found in other such houses of this period.*

LEFT *Parlor detail with period desk.*

FOLLOWING PAGES
The paneling in the dining room is not original, but has been cedar stained to replicate the original wood. It was installed from the Governor John Brooks House (now demolished) in Medford Square. This room has been mainly furnished according to the 1739 Probate Inventory of Isaac Royall Sr.

The fireplace wall in the marble chamber is a near duplicate of the one in the best room directly below. Consistent with classical rules of orders, here the pilasters have Corinthian capitals; those in the best room are Ionic. The best room is fully paneled, but this room is less expensively wallpapered.

The Slave Quarters is a substantial building of brick and clapboard that echoes the architecture of the main house. Its close proximity to the latter is consistent with practices of Northern slavery and reinforces the nature of the master-slave relationship. Such proximity facilitated both convenience and control. Slavery was abolished in Massachusetts in 1783, but this structure survives as a unique monument to the institution as practiced in Colonial New England.

The Royall family was among the richest in all of New England. As an able and important figure, Royall was promoted to brigadier general of militia in 1761. Within a decade, however, the stirrings of revolt were in the air. As a Loyalist he faced a dilemma between allegiance to home or to country, which was quickly and shockingly resolved. When at church in Boston in April 1775, British General Gage informed him and his family that their house was now behind enemy lines. The Royalls lingered in Boston for several months, then departed for Nova Scotia and from there to England, where Isaac Royall Jr. died in 1781.

Royall, however, did leave certain legacies. He endowed the Royall Professorship of Law at Harvard University. Perhaps less intentionally, he left two exceptional buildings. These give the public an opportunity to contrast the merits of wealth and privilege to poverty and slavery in eighteenth-century New England. Today the Royall House and Slave Quarters is a National Historic Landmark owned and operated by the Royall House Association.

JEREMIAH LEE MANSION

Marblehead, MA, 1767–09

LEFT *Dressed in rusticated wood ashlar, painted wet then strewn with sand to simulate limestone blocks, Lee sought a conscious imitation of English mansions of his time. The impressiveness of the house is conveyed by subdued monumentality, not the architectonic detail and contrast sought by Isaac Royall a generation before.*

OPPOSITE *The Ionic portico, so close in design to Roman and Renaissance originals, presages the wide use of this form, if not exact details, in Federal houses a generation later.*

At one time, New England was populated by various tribes of Native Americans numbering as many as the tens of thousands of English who would come to claim their land in the seventeenth century. Before that numeric invasion, however, a much more lethal one swept through their villages ravaging their lives in 1616–1619: smallpox. Introduced unseen and unrecognized by the first explorers, it decimated over ninety percent of all native inhabitants, both then and in subsequent epidemics. What happened to indigenous people in what became New England was repeated throughout the continent in decades to come. Little wonder the first settlers found the land nearly empty and the American Indians who were there mostly peaceful or at least passive, and this more out of bewilderment than sagacity.

When a few settlers at Salem chafed under the regimen of new Puritan rules, they moved in 1629 to the peninsula that became known as Marblehead (its granite shore mistaken for marble). Prospering from abundant off-shore fish, Mablehead grew into a town, separated from Salem in 1648/9 and belatedly purchased its land from the Naumkeag Indians in 1684—for sixteen pounds sterling. So rich was the fishing that fisherman from England's western counties of Devon, Dorset, Cornwall, and the Channel Islands came to settle here. Fishing became a successful industry that prospered up to the Revolution, by which time dried salt fish and all its ancillary businesses had made Marblehead approximately the tenth most populous town in the colonies.

Jeremiah Lee (1721–75) was born to a merchant family in Manchester (Cape Ann), Massachusetts. At age twenty-two he was in the bustling seaport of Marblehead where he soon married Martha Swett, the daughter of esteemed merchant Joseph Swett and sister-in-law of Robert "King" Hooper, who dominated the fish trade there for decades. Through connections and commitment, Lee began to amass one of the largest fleets in the colonies, mostly fishing schooners and trans-Atlantic brigs. While most investors owned shares of ships, Lee owned his outright. The

ABOVE *Houses are rectilinear art forms, the starkness of connected boxes partially relieved by moldings and colors. The best house designers took advantage of small opportunities to relieve the straight line by creating visual motion such as round-top windows, corner-curved banisters and, most excitingly, the drama of carved newels and balusters.*

OPPOSITE *Unlike similarly grand houses of this region and time, the elaborately paneled and carved stair-hall is not painted pine but imported Caribbean mahogany. Unmarred by cyclical fashions—change for change's sake—the Lee Mansion's mahogany is still as Lee wanted it. More like furniture than house feature, mahogany is rich in color, depth, and ability to take fine carving. The warmth of this fine wood creates a heightened aura of appreciation unmatched by any painted surfaces—no matter how well carved—in other New England houses. Such a wide hall (sixteen feet) had not been seen before in New England; the exceptionally wide stairway, however, maintains a perception of normal proportions in what is one of the grandest hallways in colonial America.*

1771 Massachusetts tax list ranked him the wealthiest person in the Commonwealth.

Equally civic, he took a leading role in Marblehead and provincial affairs, serving on local committees and in the General Court (the provincial legislature), and as a colonel of the local militia. Even before war loomed, he chose the rebel cause, serving on the secret Committees of Safety and Supplies and illegally smuggling war supplies from Europe. (His business and connections did much to facilitate the latter.) Elected to the Continental Congress, his patriot legacy was assured but for an unexpected event. On the night of Paul Revere's ride to warn of British attack (there were many other riders too that night), redcoats searched a tavern where Lee and two fellow committeemen from Marblehead were lodging for the night. They barely escaped into the night and hid. Several weeks later he succumbed to the consequences of that exposure. It was his fifty-fourth year.

Lee had begun to erect his new home in 1766, completing it in two years. After four French and Indian wars, the British had finally ousted the French, their North American nemesis, from Canada. All hoped the Peace of 1763 would usher in the first extended period of real peace and prosperity. As a result there was an explosion of construction throughout the northern colonies. Lee's house was built on an unusually large scale for its time, three stories high with an exceptionally wide central hall, with public rooms on two floors. The mass of the facade is accented by a projecting pedimented pavilion announcing the room-sized central hall. The exterior is monumental, a contrast to almost all houses of its time and place. While appearing to be of stone, it is actually of wood finished with gray sanded paint, the rusticated siding-boards shaped like dressed stone blocks. Like an English gentleman, the house is outwardly reserved, but inwardly a much more exuberant personality is expressed.

The stairway is eight-feet wide, as wide as many hallways, yet perfectly scaled to the great hallway's size. Richly carved and wainscoted in imported mahogany, it is but a prelude to a house full of paneled rooms and wallpaper. To the left of the entry hall, the best parlor fireplace is ornamented in a richly carved rococo design taken from drawings in Abraham Swan's *British Architect* (1745, plates 51 and 53). The entire room is fully paneled; the carving is unmatched in New England.

Another sumptuous room is on the second floor, a rare instance of public space at this level (although common to great houses in England). Here and in the hall (and in a second chamber opposite), Rococo ornamentation is expressed in English wallpaper paintings of Roman ruins (copied from Italian and French paintings), which Lee had ordered from London—very likely from the manufactory of William Squire.

The well-preserved quality of the house is likely the consequence of not being owned and therefore remodeled by other families. After Lee's death in 1775 it was not actively occupied until 1804, when it was purchased by Marblehead's first bank. After the bank closed a century later, the Marblehead Historical Society rescued the mansion from rumored removal of its great interior features. It is now about to enter its second century as an historic house museum, conscientiously maintained and preserved, and furnished with an outstanding collection of decorative arts.

ABOVE *After the dark mahogany sobriety—yet Rococo grandeur—of the hall and fully paneled best parlor, the family parlor is light and cheerful today, but originally it had a succession of block-printed wallpaper above the dado—light Rococo floral, Chinoiserie and mock-flock patterns. Originally its woodwork was probably beige, not today's blue. This room is conveniently positioned to the right of the front door and thus just before the kitchen. The principal dining room was across the hall, serving both for meals and for public entertainment in a period when furniture was moved to accommodate function. In this house both rooms served as parlor/dining rooms.*

OPPOSITE *In the informal parlor's fireplace are transfer-printed ceramic tiles, all with similar scenes, both monochromatic and polychrome. They were made by the manufactory of Sadler and Sadler & Green of Liverpool, England. Multicolored tiles like these were especially rare in colonial America.*

Unlike most other houses, the upper hall is as much
public space as that below. Its formal function was
announced by English wallpaper painted with scenes
of classical ruins and embellished with allegorical
trophies of architectural, pastoral, martial, and fishing
themes. Colonel Lee must have custom ordered it from
London, probably from "wallpaper stainer" William
Squire, to be hand painted en grisaille (in shades of
grays) to fit measured areas of the public rooms as
well as his own chamber. Images in the public spaces
are taken from Panini's paintings (some from French
painter Vernet) of Roman ruins made popular by
archeological excavations in the region.

ABOVE When hand-painted or block-printed wallpaper was first imported from London in the early eighteenth century, it was considered the height of fashion, but affordable by only the wealthiest. By mid-century It displaced the formerly fashionable full-height paneling above the dado in public rooms. Lee went further than others, installing hand painted Rococo scenic paper in his central stair halls and two front chambers (the only example of its type extant in it original home) and seven block-printed wallpapers in other rooms.

OPPOSITE The best chamber was probably reserved for guests and as such a public room decorated with the same scenic wallpaper as the other public spaces. Yellow silk damask replicates the original fabric used en suite for bed, window curtains and upholstery. Another rarity in colonial American homes was Lee's inventory of five carpets, apparently all English (likely Wilton) and, even more rare for the late colonial period, carpeting by the yard, to be installed wall-to-wall, and valued at twice the rate per yard as the individual carpets.

HAMILTON HOUSE

South Berwick, ME, c.1787

Salmon Falls River reaches inland by way of the Piscataqua River, of which it is a tributary. First explored in 1630, it was found rich in great stands of trees and wildlife, encouraging a settlement, now South Berwick, at the headwater of navigation on the Maine side of the river. South Berwick became the site of numerous sawmills, which brought merchants, ship builders, traders and farmers.

For native son Jonathan Hamilton (1745–1802), remembrance was a long elegiac epitaph: "Possessing those qualities which always infuse esteem: of pleasing deportment, a firm vigorous & enterprising mind . . ." Evidently esteemed by his peers, he was a Revolution captain (later colonel) of the local militia. Never mind the facts that, like others, he took advantage of the opportunity to be heavily involved in the molasses, rum, and slave trade. "His strict probity & exact punctuality secured to him the entire confidence of all that knew him, The smiles of Heaven on indefatigable industry & the blest economy rendered him eminent as a man of property."

From such perspicacity prosperity springs, including a large late Georgian house overlooking the river and his merchant wharves, warehouses, and shipbuilding yard. Built about 1785, it resembles numerous other Georgian houses of a

Facing directly down the river and overlooking his shipyard, Hamilton could watch his ships being built, depart, and return. Besides this practical convenience, siting his house so perfectly on a rise of land facing the length of river enhanced its impressiveness and thus his status in his community.

generation earlier. Hamilton was not cognizant of, or at least not comfortable with, the new Federal style. He chose his setting well, on a bluff looking down the river of his prosperity, commanding attention and respect today as if Hamilton were before us himself.

The interior is laid out with a central hall and double rooms on either side, each public room dressed in fine paneling, cornices, and arches. What is unusual is the depth of the house. Not content with a full four-square house, Hamilton increased its depth to create a rectangular parlor (and best bed chamber above) on the left of the hall, with dining room behind. On the right side was a parlor, a second stair hall, but transverse, and the kitchen behind. Presently the Tyson use of the rooms is reflected by some changes. The depth of the house accounts for the unusual height of the roof and the chimneys. Like many houses, room size and arrangement forces exterior changes, sometimes to perfection, as here, sometimes to a quandary.

Enterprise and economy usually go hand in hand. Despite Hamilton's success, after he died in 1802 his heirs suffered with a general economic decline (exacerbated by the 1807 Embargo Act) and sold the house. It was sold again three times before the Goodwin family bought it in 1839 for farming. By the end of the century New England agriculture could not compete with Mid-Western crops so the house fell into disrepair and was in danger of being leveled.

As one market declines another prospers. The Industrial Revolution, in the form of the railroads, came to the rescue. A new class of wealthy New Englanders sought out colonial houses as summer retreats. Emily Tyson, widow of the president of the Baltimore and Ohio Railroad, bought the tired old house and, with her stepdaughter Elise Tyson (later Vaughn) set out to restore the house in the Colonial Revival manner. They had been drawn to this "quiet place that the destroying hand of progress had failed to touch" by local authoress Sarah Orne Jewett who had loved it from youth and made it the setting of one of her novels, *The Tory Lover*. Sharing Jewett's respect for the house's past, the Tysons retained what was original, added a kitchen wing on the east side of the house and sleeping porches on the west (later removed), moved the Goodwin's barn and created splendid gardens.

Celebrating the 1876 Centennial of our country's birth proved a wellspring of nostalgia for decades as Americans sought to recreate or restore visual settings of a glorious patrimony. The Colonial Revival appeared, then and even now, in many variations. Countless colonial style houses were built, while long-neglected early houses, like Hamilton's, were given rebirth with varying sensitivity to a real or imaged past. Jonathan Hamilton's house is one of the most successful houses to undergo this transformation because the new owners recognized and preserved Hamilton's work while accommodating their needs with a light touch.

ABOVE AND OPPOSITE *The principal parlor has paired window alcoves much like those in the Isaac Royall House (p. 44) of forty years before. Hamilton was content to use what was becoming* retardé *Georgian, comfortably fitting into the style of other houses in this upriver community. The murals by Fernold, 1907, show houses of Portsmouth, as well as Thomas Jefferson's Monticello.*

FOLLOWING PAGES *The dining room's murals define its Colonial Revival theme. George Porter Fernald painted the murals in 1905 with Italian gardens, villas, grottoes, and hillside villages, the reminder of favorite jaunts he shared with the Tysons.*

Before the modern era of multifunction rooms, a "chamber" was a private room for sleeping, usually on the second floor, the province of the chambermaid. Before mechanical cleaning, cooking, and transport devices, maintaining a large house was as complex as a business. Little wonder wives were chatelaines of the household, supervising maids, cooks, butlers, gardeners, liverymen, and more. Her chamber became the last refuge from responsibility, a private setting for contemplation as well as rest.

FOLLOWING PAGES *The parlor chamber nearly duplicates the woodwork of the room below, only the fireplace enframement and cornice dentilation is simplified.*

The property had been used as a farm through much of the nineteenth century so when Mrs. Tyson acquired it, all vestiges of any gardens Hamilton may have had were gone. She used her sense for the Colonial to create new gardens, an artful and pleasing combination of older formal arrangements with ornaments and the color of perennial flowerbeds.

HARRISON GRAY OTIS HOUSE

Boston, MA, 1795

LEFT *"The Brick House," as Otis called it, was fully developed Federal style in 1796, when designed by his friend Charles Bulfinch, but chaste in detail, its visual impact carried by a grid of well-spaced vertical openings and horizontal marble banding, all contrasted against brick. In 1926 The Society for the Preservation of New England Antiquities (or SPNEA, and now Historic New England) moved what was then its headquarters building forty feet to save it during the widening of Cambridge Street.*

OPPOSITE *The front entry's delicate features are almost exactly replicated on the inside. Although appearing as if a double door in the French fashion, it is actually single since it lacked width for the former yet preserved its intended elegance.*

If geography is destiny, the Shawmut Peninsula was ground zero for the Puritans in 1630. It was the tongue of a giant-mouth harbor, the largest and finest in New England. The village was named Boston after the Lincolnshire town many had come from. Puritan ethics established a stable and structured base for expansion, starting with America's first public school (Boston Latin, 1635) and college (Harvard, 1636). Boston grew inexorably into the economic, political, educational, and cultural center of the region, made hallowed by its seminal role in the Revolution.

In New England we note how often opportunity and responsibility go hand-in-hand. So many who did well for themselves, did well for others, both in war and peace. Harrison Gray Otis (1765–1848) of Boston matured quickly through difficult political times, realizing lawyering was the way to means and meaning. His father was in the Confederation Congress in 1787–88 and secretary of the U.S. Senate from its first session in 1789 until his

death. Precocious young Otis graduated from Harvard at age eighteen, was admitted to the bar in 1786, entered private practice and became a Federalist in what proved to be a long public career. Successively he was a member of the Massachusetts State House of Representatives, 1796; U.S. district attorney for Massachusetts, 1796; U.S. representative from Massachusetts at-large, 1797–1801; member of Massachusetts State Senate, 1805; state court judge in Massachusetts, 1814; U.S. senator from Massachusetts, 1817–22; and mayor of Boston, 1829–31. Being so frequently away, his wife Sally handled his business, kept the accounts, and collected the rents, as well as cared for their four children.

For his family Otis went top drawer, using the fortune he made developing Beacon Hill to hire leading architect and friend Charles Bulfinch to design and build three successive Federal-style houses in Boston (1795, 1801, 1806), each one larger than the last, each in newly fashionable neighborhoods created by Otis and his partners. The first being this one, "in point of elegance and

ABOVE *The withdrawing room's mantle, wallpaper and paper border—reflecting the best English taste of the period—all play to the appeal of flowers, suggesting pleasure gardens, although we do not know of such in the Otis's time.*

OPPOSITE *The withdrawing room was planned as the most elegant room in the house and, at that, on the second floor. It once had an imported marble mantle and may have displayed the best of Otis' collection of Old Master paintings. Four panels of each door were inset with mirrors in the interest of reflected light.*

situation not inferior to any Estate in Boston." It is said to have been inspired by Bulfinch's observation of the William Bingham house in Philadelphia (c.1785). In plan it has a center hall with two rooms on either side, the kitchen relegated to an ell. It is three stories high (the upper story of low ceilings for servants), and five bays wide with an entrance portico added in 1801. A Palladian window (though in fact it was originated by Serlio) is a holdover from the prior Georgian style but the lunette above is in the new Federal style.

As fashionable Bostonians moved to new developments, elegant houses like Otis' were left behind, surviving thanks to new owners, tenants, and boarders. Visionary William Sumner Appleton, founder of the Society for the Preservation of New England Antiquities (now better known as Historic New England), had the society acquire the Otis House as its headquarters in 1916. Meticulously recording its social and structural changes, the house's phases of restoration have resulted in a stunning evocation of what Federal architecture was all about.

LEFT *While evolving out of the Georgian style, Federal features, such as stair balusters, are thinner, creating a visual lightness and grace. The robust spiral Georgian newel post is now a delicate group of balusters.*

OPPOSITE *The upper hall, while trimmed in fine moldings and plasterwork, is decidedly subdued in colors. The use of the so-called Palladian window (actually first used by the architect's predecessor Serlio) was, by this time, being replaced by the elliptical arched window. Interior shutter windows, as seen here, were normal in the finer Georgian and Federal houses, usefully protecting valuable fabrics from the sun, keeping the house cooler on warm sunny days, warmer on cold sunless days, and relieving the intrusion of winter cold nights.*

GENERAL GEORGE COWLES HOUSE

Farmington, CT, 1803–08

This is a house of unexpectedly innovative merit. Its entrance faces the street in the near universal manner (opposite), yet its principal facade (left), which faces the garden, does not. For once, here is a house whose greatest pleasures are reserved for private, not public enjoyment. The facade it presents to the garden is extraordinary: two twelve-foot-high floors framed by a five columned pedimented portico. Mistaken for Greek Revival by most, it is in fact, Roman Revival, within the domain of Thomas Jefferson's architectural gift to the young republic he had given documentary birth to years before.

Hartford, at the head of navigation on the Connecticut River, was first settled by Dutch who claimed all the land from there to the Hudson River. It was a timid, insupportable claim, however, since New Englanders soon moved to the area at what is now Hartford, Windsor, and Wethersfield. In 1640 a dozen families moved off from those towns to the fertile bottom-lands along the Farmington River to the west, which they purchased from the Tunxis Indians. For a century, farming was the mainstay that attracted others. Because of the large, original landholding, the town spawned several others before and after the Revolution. By then the village had earned a reputation for fine houses. Washington, passing through in 1780 and 1781, commented on "the village of pretty houses." In the latter year an officer under the command of Comte de Rochambeau wrote, "This town contains some of the handsomest houses and best people in America." Pride and great patriots have proved to be our earliest inspiration for preservation.

Farmington is still a town of stylish period houses, but not just from farming. By the time of the Revolution, proverbial Yankee ingenuity had built new opportunities in manufacturing linen, leather goods, muskets, and buttons. Prosperity spawned investment in homes and their contents as the town attracted cabinetmakers, silversmiths, weavers, carriage builders, and many other trades. With a river to the sea and new freedom to trade anywhere, Farmington became a trading center sending products to the South, and importing from as far away as China.

In 1802, merchant and trader Solomon Cowles (1758–1814) gave 14 acres and this new-built Federal house to his son George Cowles (1780–1860) "for consideration of the parental affection which I have for my son," and, in commemoration of his marriage to Abigail Derning on December 3, 1803. Young Cowles carried on his father's mercantile business but was apparently more active in the state militia, raising to the top rank of major general. When he died in 1860 he left the house to his sons, his widow

receiving life tenancy. Son James retained the house until 1907 when he sold it to Theodate Pope (1868–1946), architect, Farmington resident (though she never lived in this house), and designer of her family's extensive estate Hill-Stead (p. 196). Content to maintain the house with little changes (though adding four units of worker housing), she sold it in 1944. Architect James McA. Thompson bought it in 1963, reversing some later changes during a restoration, which resulted in elegant furnishings and finishes. On his death it came under the protection of the SPNEA (Society for the Preservation of New England Antiquities) and was sold with protective covenants to the present owners who have continued an unbroken line of sensitive stewardship, preserving one of the most unusual of Federal houses in New England, although two houses in nearby Hartford, long demolished, were similar.

The house has a number of noteworthy features that suggest a relationship to Thomas Jefferson's brand of Classical Revival. Although an architect has not been identified for this house,

Solomon Cowles had business in the south and may have been acquainted with its new architecture. The imposing pedimented portico of five thirty-foot Ionic columns faces the garden, not the public way. The columns are stuccoed brick in the southern manner, not wood. The porch is raised on a brick vaulted base with ground level entrance to the cellar; the effect is a south facade that towers over the landscape. The parlor windows extend to the floor; when raised (into a space in the brick wall above), they give convenient egress onto the porch and garden view. The front entrance is on the east facade facing the street. It opens into a dramatic two-story stairwell lit by a Palladian window on each floor of the long staircase, each similar to the window in the tympanum triangle of the south pediment. Both floors are a breathtaking twelve feet high; the parlor and dining room are finished in fine moldings and mantles, in the manner of Scottish architect Robert Adams, whose books and houses show the influence of a rediscovered appreciation of Roman villa design.

Great houses inspire great gardens, as a beautiful face invites fine jewelry. Being organic, gardens change with the season and through the years, yet continue to be inspired by the face—the facades—of the home. Classical ornaments continue to decorate the surrounding gardens of the Cowles house.

GARDNER-PINGREE HOUSE

Salem, MA, 1804–05

LEFT *Front facade of the Gardner-Pingree House.* Photograph Courtesy of the Peabody Essex Museum, Salem, MA.

OPPOSITE *A king without a crown is a mere mortal; a house without cornice is a box. McIntire's inspired aesthetics added more: an elliptical portico deftly mirroring the broad transom light of John Gardner's home. If there be perfection in style, this is it for Federal.*

The rich fishing grounds of New England were the base from which Salem village grew into a major port—its fleets sailing "To the Farthest port of the rich east," as its motto proclaims. By the end of the Revolution it was one of the larger cities in the country, built upon port trading, especially with China for tea, cod to Europe and the West Indies, and deriving sugar, molasses, and slaves from the latter. If peace brought prosperity, war did too. Privateering, the officially sanctioned raiding of enemy commerce on the seas during the Revolution and War of 1812, added wealth to trade, supplying the means for great houses of the Georgian and Federal periods.

John Gardner was from a Salem family in the import-export business. Sending out his twelve-ship fleet, he received from Europe, India, and South America exotic cargoes which he sold to the newly rich of Massachusetts, creating a large fortune. He was also prominent in civic affairs, serving as a selectman and on numerous Salem committees. By 1804, ready for a house fitting

his station, he commissioned Samuel McIntire to build a large brick Federal house on Essex Street.

Samuel McIntire (1757–1811) was the native son for whom the town's historic district is aptly named. He was the remarkably talented designer and builder of many of Salem's Federal houses, including their decorations and furnishings. Raised in a family of Salem housewrights, he and his brothers were in business from 1779 creating Georgian houses for local merchants; then, within a decade, Samuel began creating houses in the more refined Federal style of which Gardner's house has been considered his finest and last achievement, a tribute to McIntire's great sense for proportions and decorative detailing. Some of his finest examples of woodcarving are to be seen on the mantles, doorframes, and on the Corinthian capitols supporting the semicircular front portico. McIntire's carving talent extended to sophisticated furniture in the Hepplewhite and Sheraton style, decorated with his distinctive carved motifs, several examples being in the house. While he

If Georgian architecture reads solid rectilinial mass, Federal reads light-footed curvilinear motion. Like his furniture, McIntire's house features fairly dance in implied visual motion as if "rose-lipped maidens . . . light foot lads."

Until the age of modern "central" (actually distributive) heat there was a persistent contradiction expressed in domestic architecture: the need to economically heat separate rooms yet entertain in large spaces. The double pocket door nearly solved this dilemma in larger Georgian to Greek Revival houses (thereafter the house opened up thanks to furnaces). The twin parlors of Gardner's house could hold a host of guests who no doubt created as much warmth as the fireplaces.

In any house the one spot that creates "life"—the fire hearth—is also the darkest and dirtiest; life and consuming death in one action, deftly symbolized by the Phoenix bird of ancient legend appropriately depicted on some hearth firebacks. Like a picture frame, mantles give prominence to this fire box, distracting attention from the gaping black hole in warm months. McIntire's creative genius was less as a carver (many could do fine copy work) than as a sculptor of forms to live with: furniture, mantles, and houses to live in. The Gardner-Pingree house is perhaps his finest work and one of the nation's highest achievements in the Federal style.

FOLLOWING PAGES *Regardless of season the kitchen was always warm. In summer, however, it became too hot, inspiring many owners to create summer kitchens in cellars, wings or separate structures away from habitation rooms. In this case the main kitchen incorporates a roasting oven, the result of the recent heating/ cooking innovations of New Hampshire born Benjamin Thompson, later honored as Count Rumford.*

was self-taught, he achieved the status of a first-rate architect, partly from borrowing ideas from architects Charles Bulfinch and Asher Benjamin, but as much from his own innate artistic talent. No one could produce decorative work as finely as he could.

He died in 1811, the same year in which Gardner, having suffered serious financial reversals (as had occurred to so many ship owners and traders because of the 1807 Embargo Act), sold his house. Salem would see a revival, but its glory days were about over. The next owner was no more tenured than Gardner, who sold it to Captain Joseph White in 1814. White had the pleasure of sixteen years there before being murdered, a shocking event which inspired Nathaniel Hawthorne, ever intrigued by the dark side of Salem history, to write about it in the short story "Mr. Higginbotham's Catastrophe." Then for a century the Pingree family lived there, apparently contentedly, for they donated it to the Essex Institute.

OPPOSITE *The roles of "light" in architecture are manifold, allowing for illumination and the refinement of mass and detail—features seamlessly matched in Federal design. One purpose of "light" is to inspire the psyche, to enliven the mind; no better achieved than in this hall where high ceilings, delicate balusters, and an infusion of sunlight combine to "let there be light."*

RIGHT *These bedrooms reflect the ageless quest to achieve harmony and balance with form and color. The persistent popularity or revival of past interior style-ways is a credit to how well our forebears worked out the range of attractive possibilities; unlike science, art is not cumulative, it is inspired afresh in each individual out of unfathomable depths of subconscious intuition.*

GORE PLACE
THE CHRISTOPHER GORE HOUSE

Waltham, MA, 1805–06

Christopher Gore (1758–1827) was one of thirteen children of a successful Boston paint merchant and color shop owner who was able to send his son to Harvard College. Graduating in 1776, young Gore entered the army as a clerk in his future brother-in-law's regiment (his Loyalist father had fled to Canada). At the end of the war he apprenticed in a law office, and then opened his own in Boston. It was a fortuitous time to be a lawyer in Boston. So many of the old lawyers had been Tories and left the city to a new generation. Post-war Boston was wealthy, extending opportunities for the ambitious. Gore, like some other lawyers, was as much an investor as an advocate, adding to his wealth by purchasing revolutionary scrip and investing in new mills and toll roads. He married Rebecca Amory Payne in 1785, daughter of a wealthy merchant and maritime insurer. The couple purchased land in Waltham, the site of a future country seat.

Gore's career had a public side. At age thirty, he was elected Boston's representative to the Philadelphia convention to ratify

The Gores' residence and travels in Europe while planning this house explains something of why the result seemed so unusual to New Englanders when it was erected in 1805–6. The long paired wings (and lunette windows) go back to Palladio's sixteenth-century villas, adapted by the English in later centuries. The elliptical main block is also English eighteenth-century fashion; the floor-length windows French inspirations (those of three parts cleverly adapted from a Federal doorway form). A low octagonal cupola (not the room-size crown of its southern counterpart at Monticello) modestly serves interior lighting. Jefferson would have enjoyed the Gores' creation.

The east entry hall. No doubt all generations since have shared with the Gores a delight in the dramatic. Stairways, so conceived, are the dynamic sculpture of domestic architecture. What better place than on a stairway to meet on equal terms, face to face, past residents. Of all house furnishings, portraits are left for the future to remember the past. Unnecessary while the subject lived, these images are icons of immortality, there for friends and family to remember and yet those unborn to be inspired.

The first floor parlor, enlivened with Chinese-style wallpaper of exotic flowers and birds, was entered from either the east entry hall, great hall, or the oval drawing room. To the right, men passed to the billiard r oom in the wing. From end to end the house is 170-feet long, of which Gore ruefully commented "the great objection is in its dimensions—it is too large for our family, and though built with economy, and perfect freedom from ornament, will cost me more money, than will suit my love of ease and indulgence . . ."

LEFT *Federal mantles of the better sort, as here in the great hall, were not mere molded frames for fireplaces but could illustrate allegorical allusions, often drawing on classical tales or metaphorical icons. This one depicts the hunt, an ancient pastime for developing skills required for war.*

OPPOSITE *The oval drawing room is the central room of the garden facade, its tall windows taking in the Gores' extensive landscape. Fifteen-feet high, its outsized form, features and shape owe their inspiration to the Gores' travels in England and France. It has also served as the dining room.*

ABOVE *To the west of the great hall and closer to the basement kitchens, is an intimate dining space with noticeably lower ceilings.*

OPPOSITE *In the east wing pavilion was Gore's Library of which one visitor wrote "The Library and other apartments display a love and knowledge of the Fine Arts..." To the right is a door to the bathing chamber (not shown). In Gore's account book of 1806 he recorded purchasing a bathing apparatus used as a therapeutic treatment for his arthritic knees.*

the new United States Constitution. He must have caught President Washington's eye, for Washington appointed him the first United States attorney for Massachusetts. In 1793 Gore built a sizable house at Waltham. The president then appointed him, in 1796, to John Jay's commission to negotiate claims against Britain for war losses. While away, their newly built Waltham house burned to the ground (the carriage barn survives today). The next design appears to reflect their travels to great country houses and the influence of Sir John Soane in London and Parisian architect Jacques-Guillaume Legrand, the latter being asked to make a "... compleat [sic] & perfect plan according to our sketch."

The new mansion was under construction within the year of their return in 1804. Composed of a two-story central block and one story wings, it has more in common with southern houses, like Jefferson's Monticello, than anything in New England. It had a number of innovate conveniences: a bathing apparatus, water closet, a laundry drying chamber, and a kitchen equipped with a "Rumford Roaster," likely learned from Rumford who they had met in France. Eschewing ornamentation, the house's elegance derives from refined proportions and reserved but high quality details. With remarkable energy, as soon as the house was finished, Gore ran for the Massachusetts Senate and a year later for governor (on the third try, in 1809, he was elected). Four years later he was appointed to the US Senate, spending three years in Washington before retiring to Waltham in declining health. Now their house was to become a year-round residence, requiring "double windows" in four rooms, installing woolen carpets and improvements to the heating and cooling systems.

The house was designed for and used in a public way. A sidelight on the Gores' social life is suggested by their employment of Robert Roberts, an accomplished butler of African-American origin, active in Boston's abolitionist movement, who, in the year Gore died, wrote and published *The House Servant's Directory*, a manual codifying rules and guidelines for domestics.

Gore Place has recently been undergoing a careful restoration and now displays many features and furnishings from the Gore period. The broad landscape hints at the extensive well-managed farm and pleasure grounds the Gores had created. Surrounded by a plantation of trees, it contained, within cultivated fields, fruit, and kitchen gardens, a fruit nursery and orchard, bridle paths, pond, and large greenhouses. When the home lot of 33-plus acres was put up for sale at Rebecca Gore's death in 1834 it was described in an advertisement from the *Boston Daily Advertiser* as being "in perfect repair, equally calculated for a winter or summer residence, and in taste, style, and convenience exceeded by none in the country ..."

ABOVE *The house's two-story central block contains five chambers: three facing the landscape; this one and another face the entry facade.*

RIGHT *The sitting room, in the oval center of the second floor, has a panoramic view over the garden and grounds.*

RUNDLET-MAY HOUSE

Portsmouth, NH, 1807

James Rundlet (1772–1852) was the son of a farming family from Exeter New Hampshire who, at age twenty-two, came down to Portsmouth to seek a livelihood. This he achieved quite quickly as a commission merchant dealing in textiles. Within a few years he had amassed a considerable amount of money by which he bought a large lot, though not in the settled part of the town. There he built what he called his "Manshon House" in 1807–8, thought to have been designed by his own hand. Good houses, of course, are not built without precedent; Rundlet had likely been impressed by Samuel McIntire's 1804 masterpiece in Salem, the Gardner-Pingee House (p. 102), whose facade in brick and marble is so like Rundlet's, in wood. While substantial in size, being three-stories high and five-bays wide, his Federal details are tasteful but reserved. This suggests Rundlet had one eye for establishing his social position in the community, while the other was clearly on functional matters.

While prudent, he reached for fine quality furnishings. Imported English wallpaper, glassware, ceramics, and furniture by fine Portsmouth makers. Some pieces, by well-known Langley Boardman, are still to be seen in the house. Several pieces hint at a Federal affection for strong colors: white painted fancy chairs, another

The front elevation of the Rundlet-May house. Here, as Frost's articulation of native wisdom attests, fences make good neighbors. They define public from private space, metaphorically for people, graphically for animals. They announce the ancient concept of private property rights, a cornerstone of capitalism. Beautiful fences are like lovely people, they hide their raw purposes with the welcoming distraction of a light and airy facade; you may see and enjoy but to not trespass.

126

ABOVE *Entry hall.*

RIGHT *In September of 1809 Jane and James Rundlet's choice of wallpaper was installed, an English "Peach Damask" with a "Paris Flock" border. Two centuries of family and museum pride in its builder have preserved the wallpaper intact.*

LEFT *Detail of fine wood furniture carving typical of the period.*

OPPOSITE *Were once Georgian fireplace walls were flanked with dish-holding cupboards, Federal parlors now have the welcome light of more windows, the dishes banished to new pantries in a creative flurry of new-function spaces.*

FOLLOWING PAGES *Rundlet had a flair for the new and practical, incorporating inventions as they became available. He installed the latest in kitchen cooking and heating technology after the theories of Count Rumford. The kitchen still retains a Rumford roaster, an oven in which meat is roasted, moistened and tenderized by steam generated from its juices, then allowed to brown by letting the steam out. By ingenious ducting of fire flues a roast is heated evenly all around, eliminating the need for rotation. Two centuries later we are yet to achieve this level of sophistication. More than that, there is a Rumford range with inset kettles, each with its own firebox, separately regulated, producing hot water for coffee, tea, food preparation and cooking. In the scullery there is a large kettle next to the fireplace to produce hot water for laundry and washing, any wastewater draining out into the service yard. The fireplace flue is directed to a third floor smoke chamber to cure meat. Additional attached out-buildings provided sheltered areas for several more household functions, including a privy with flocked wallpaper.*

set of red painted fancy chairs, and painted and gilt curtain poles. The account books record seven types of imported wallpaper of which a "Peach Damask" with "Paris Flock Border" are in the parlor, and original samples of "Green Net" and "Green Worm," more attractive by eye than ear, survive, but "Gothic stair case Paper," "drab and green" fabric, and carpeting, all ordered at that time, are now missing.

Rundlet paid equal attention to his land, grading terraces around the house and installing flowerbeds, shrub rows, a kitchen garden, and orchard, all lined with paths and fences. No doubt his own farming experience was the master of this design.

We know so much about the property because Rundlet kept meticulous account books, which survive. We don't know much about Rundlet as a person, however, except what speaks through his account books and the property itself. His obituary, however, is revealing of how others saw him. The house was "imposing in appearance and an object of envy to many who predicted with wise nods that so much pride must have a fall and concluded that he had built his house too high—but they happened to have been

Rundlet's high-style Portsmouth furniture of contrasting colors and figured maple against somber mahogany, are themselves a contrast to generations of conservative family use and modest additions.

FOLLOWING PAGES *The value of a home long held by the same family is its self-commentary on generational taste and means. Preservation museums, like the families of which they are now custodians, instruct more of social history than designed taste; of a families' fortunes more than cultural acumen. An architect and his patron may set the stage for the first performance, subsequent acts are more a matter of personal choices than professional inspiration.*

mistaken." The farm boy did well, and made it stick—for two centuries. An early observer sensed how Rundlet and his house were expressions of each other when he said "his house was built large enough and built right, stands unaltered and needing no alterations, having lasted out the lifetime of the owner . . . and bidding fair to Outlast other generations. . . ."

A remarkable quality of this house is the fact that it remained in the family until recent times, a family that kept possessions and made few changes. It is indeed a preservation museum, not a restoration, for it preserves generations of one family's lifestyle. After three generations the house was given to SPNEA (The Society for the Preservation of New England Antiquities) in 1973 by Ralph May, the great-grandson of the builder. He and his mother had assiduously tracked down family heirlooms in other branches of the related Rundlet, May, and Morrison families, which accounts for the unusual number of pieces in the house, more than James Rundlet likely contemplated.

ABOVE *Salvia, lilies, and petunias bloom in the west-facing garden.*

RIGHT *The west elevation of the house with a glimpse of the attached outbuildings and garden.*

BROOKSIDE
THE WILCOX-CUTTS HOUSE

Orwell, VT, 1835

Vermont is the far northwest corner of New England. Originally a part of New Hampshire (but partly claimed by New York), it became a state in 1791. Its location had much to do with its late settlement. Vermont's western border is the lengthy Lake Champlain, a fertile valley region but during most of the colonial period it served as the invasion route between French and British North America, no boon to settlement until France lost Canada in 1763. The town of Orwell is in Addison County near the lower west border with New York, just across a narrow neck of Lake Champlain from Fort Ticonderoga.

The beginning of the farm that would become known as Brookside was a grant of land from the New Hampshire governor Benning Wentworth in 1766 to land speculators Benjamin Walker and Gifford Daily, who, in 1788, sold off the portion on which the house would be built to W. H. William Holenbeck. He cleared the land and erected a house and barns, which still stand. Yet he sold the farm and 128 acres in 1798 to Ebenezer Wilcox, a man with ambition on his mind.

Born in Connecticut, Wilcox had moved in 1793 to Newport, New Hampshire, where he married Thankful Stevens. Her sister was married to an original settler of Orwell, Vermont, which may account for the Wilcoxes settling upon the farm there.

Commanding the high ground like its Greek temple inspiration, Linus Wilcox's deeply colonnaded home overlooks the expansive Lake Champlain valley. His talented builder, James Lamb, no doubt created his masterpiece thanks to the support and indulgence of his patron. With balanced wings set behind protective columned loggias, it is a sight to be admired from any distance.

As if hanging in mid-air, the spiraling staircase Thomas Dake, "House-Joiner," created for Wilcox is as fluid an example of a solid possible in architecture, only its attachment to the wall anchors it from a fear of unsafe assent. The gold leaf was inspired by original Chinese tea-chest paper once discovered to have been there. The stairway, like all woods of the house is from the farm, in this case butternut over oak. Grand staircases are universally admired—daughters' weddings often their justification—as they present a regal platform for receiving guests, as much as a monarch descending from a throne. For the designer and craftsmen it is a singular advertisement of creative achievement. Of course for children it is the original entertainment center, to every mother's horror.

Wilcox undertook extensive improvements, expanding the acres, moving and enlarging the house, building a large milking shed and adjoining buttery. He created a park and gardens with many exotic trees and shrubs. After 1810 he was able to get some scarce Spanish Merino sheep (Spain had tried to keep a monopoly on this breed), noted for their fine fleece, which revolutionized the wool industry by producing fine quality wool clothing. Wilcox and his son Linus made a fortune breeding the sheep and exporting them to Australia. A single prized breeding ram was reported to be worth $15,000.

Linus (1799–1868) inherited the farm in 1834 and nine years later had local master builder James Lamb (1810–1871) build a large Greek Revival home based in part, as is so often the case in rural America at this time, on the published pattern books of Asher Benjamin and Minard Lafever. It was unusually large (87 1/2-by-35 feet) with sophisticated woodwork (using seven species from the farm) and was said to have cost $30,000. The old house became a wing to the new. The house must have contributed positively to Lamb's reputation for he went on to build many more houses in the region.

From the 1850s it was known as Brookside Stock Farm. Linus had married twice and by his second wife had children; the first-born, Rollin (1835–1872) inherited the farm briefly in 1868, before leaving it to his sister Corneila Wilcox Cutts (1839–1929). She and her husband Henry moved their Morgan horse stud farm to Brookside, adding a large stable and half-mile track and grandstand for training and showing their trotters (J. P. Morgan visited at least twice and bought a dozen Morgan horses). The farm continued with Merino sheep and added Duroc swine and an extensive apple orchard of many varieties. By the next generation however, the advent of the automobile made Morgan horses obsolete and the Depression finished the farm's prosperity. In 1942 it was sold, and since then has had five owners who have tastefully restored the house and grounds, especially the present owners. Today it is a large working farm raising Belted Galloway cattle, hay, corn, vegetables, fruits, and Maple Syrup, while also being an elegant bed and breakfast establishment.

LEFT *If the temple format has limitations, it also has advantages. The front room has a panorama of windows taking in the wide landscape while the overhanging porch shades them from noonday sun. A coffered ceiling and pilaster supports for a deep entablature are rarely seen embellishments for a country Greek Revival house.*

OPPOSITE *Making the most of native woods, the gallery's visual drama comes from the stark contrast of stained and natural birch on the parquet floor and walnut and gold leaf on the trim. Another native inspiration is the interconnected doorframes, with a full-length mirror between cleverly suggesting an identical room beyond. Large pier mirrors as space enhancers a la Versailles' Hall of Mirrors were a vogue in mid-nineteenth century America.*

FOLLOWING PAGES *The original house, a modest Federal farm house on the property, was apparently moved to its present site as an "L" for the new house, the original kitchen becoming the new dining room, likely an accommodation to the space limitations imposed by keeping the new house within its strict temple format.*

ABOVE *A secondary chamber with ample light and windows allows for quiet contemplation of the landscape beyond.*

RIGHT *The parlor chamber (master bedroom in today's parlance) enjoys the same panoramic views as the parlor below. The Grecian-style door and window surrounds conveniently provide space for a carved adaptation of a Greek motif, an anthemion, accented by blue as if glazed terra cotta inserts.*

FOLLOWING PAGES *Ancient Greek columns are found in different forms and orders, those here are of the graceful Ionic order with spiral capitals, turned base and attenuated tapered columns. The ancients long discovered that the weightless beauty of a column is created by its taper, what they called entasis, the lower third straight to convey solidity, the upper part gradually tapered by time-honored formula to relieve the appearance of mass to convey effortless strength.*

148

JUSTIN S. MORRILL HOMESTEAD

Strafford, VT, 1848

I n the countryside of east-central Vermont is a crossroads where the small village of Strafford is to be found, little changed and gracefully preserved from its founding in 1761, when New Hampshire Governor Benning Wentworth granted a town charter (as well as many other townships, although New York claimed much of what later became Vermont). Settlement began during the Revolutionary War, followed by one of the earliest copper mines in the United States (1793, continuing until 1958). The upper village of Strafford is crowned by the stately 1791 Strafford Town House constructed atop a man-made hill at the head of the Town Common. The Gothic Revival Morrill Homestead is located on a hillside at the lower end of the village.

Justin Smith Morrill (1810–98) was born and raised in Strafford, Vermont, of a family of modest means who could not afford for him the benefit of higher education. At age fifteen be began working as a merchant's clerk in Strafford and later in Portland, Maine. By 1831 he was back in Strafford as a merchant, a career he pursued with singular success, allowing him to retire at age thirty-eight in 1848 to concentrate on other business interests in agriculture and horticulture. Intellectually curious despite a lack of formal education, he became self-educated in business, archi-

In Morrill's library is a copy of A. J. Downing's Cottage Residences *(1844) in which the author espoused his design for "A Villa in the Rural Gothic style," adding this persuasion: "We have designed this villa to express the life of a family of refined and cultivated taste, full of home feeling, love for the country, and enjoyment of the rural and beautiful in nature—and withal, a truly American home, in which all is adapted to the wants and habits of life of a family in independent circumstances." Morrill apparently found the plan and characterization irresistible.*

OPPOSITE *Trefoils and quatrefoils, like cloverleaves, hark back to the close-to-nature naturalness of medieval architecture. That is how A. J. Davis and A. J. Downing, the high priests of Gothic Revival in rural America, saw their calling—build what fits the setting congenially and you shall also have a harmonious life. The Gothic Revival mined a staggering assortment of cottage-to-cathedral motifs, yet its initial popularity as a style was short lived. After the Civil War, elements of the Gothic continued to resurface in house designs which masquerade under other titles: Late Gothic, Carpenter Gothic, Stick Style, Queen Anne, Tudor, Shingle Style and Arts and Crafts.*

RIGHT *Fame is relative to circumstances. Of modest origin, the self-made man had, for posterity, the good luck of being the greatest man of his small town. Honored by association, Morrill's country home became a town shrine, a beacon to inspire others to greatness. In a large city his house would have been forgotten if not lost to urban renewal. Today the parlor is the perfectly preserved embodiment of pre–Civil War domesticity, little changed by Morrill, his family, and those since, who have revered his memory.*

LEFT *In days prior to such modern amenities as television and radio, "home entertainment" was produced in the home. Common pastimes included the playing of musical instruments, singing, and storytelling.*

OPPOSITE *Castellated door and window heads reference not only a medieval past but the then current romantic passion for chivalrous literature. Wall-to-wall carpeting, generally associated with the Victorian period, was actually common to better quality Federal homes, and even some Georgian. Besides its contribution to decoration, carpeting lent at least a feeling for warmth on cold days. In many houses they were removed in summer, replaced by woven rattan matting, also wall-to-wall.*

OPPOSITE *Although picture galleries date back to at least the sixteenth century in England, Morrill's gallery-cum-library must have been viewed as a curiosity in rural Vermont, the product of an inquisitive mind and acquisitive personality. Collecting objects d'art for their own sake, not just for decoration, became a passion still indulged in today. Morrill's use of colored windows for light and design found later parallels in Arts and Crafts and Frank Lloyd Wright's Prairie style homes.*

RIGHT *The art of glass enameling, not really stained, dates back a millennium. By the mid-nineteenth century it reached a sophistication unmatched except by paintings and had superior luminosity. For Morrill's gallery it added a new form of representational art, as aesthetically pleasing and intellectually informative as his prints and paintings.*

159

The Morrill Homestead's pantry is at once functional, neat, and amply lit by natural illumination.

FOLLOWING PAGES
LEFT *Second-story hall.*

RIGHT TOP *Before efficient heating systems, bedrooms became cold at night when fires went out; curtain beds helped retain body heat. By the Civil War coal furnaces kept warmth more constant and so beds could and did become open and ornamental. By Morrill's time bedroom furniture was often made of fancy painted sets, made to match or decoratively painted to match. Such "cottage furniture" was locally made and relatively inexpensive, its best quality derived from the facile charm of its decoration.*

BOTTOM RIGHT *Fine quality bedroom sets were produced in hardwoods, some with marble tops, the better to clean and avoid spoiling shellacked wood surfaces.*

tecture, agriculture, horticulture, and politics. He designed and built his Gothic Revival house (1848–51) in Strafford. Politics became his legacy from the time of his election to the U.S. House of Representatives in 1854 as a Whig (and subsequently as a Republican), followed by the U.S. Senate in 1867, serving continuously until his death in 1898.

In Washington, he had the architect of the Capitol build him a mansion on Thomas Circle, his birthday parties being a highlight of the social season each year. Even today his portrait hangs just outside the Senate Chamber, wherein his colleagues in the 1890s respectfully honored him with the title "Father of the Senate."

He was a skilled behind-the-scenes negotiator; as chairman of the House Ways and Means Committee he engineered the first national income tax to help fund the Civil War.

His greatest renown came as chief sponsor of the Morrill Acts (Land Grant College Acts) of 1862 and 1890, the most important educational legislation of the nineteenth-century, which established land grant colleges in all states for the liberal and practical education of farmers, mechanics, artisans, and laborers, funded by the sale of seventeen-million acres of Federal land. These acts established for the first time practical training in science, agriculture, and engineering, and, also for the first time, provided America's working class and minority citizens the opportunity to pursue higher education. Parenthetically, he sponsored the Morrill Anti-Bigamy Act of 1862, outlawing polygamy (a Mormon practice).

Morrill was a throwback to an earlier era before architects, when gentlemen designed their homes with the aid of housewrights. His rosy pink Gothic Revival house attests to his accomplished self-education, which also extended to the farm's grounds, which he designed in the popular picturesque landscape manner. In his private library were A. J. Downing's and other popular books advocating the architectural style and landscape design Morrill adopted. The seventeen-room house retains the features he designed, as well as furnishings that were family possessions.

VICTORIA MANSION
THE MORSE-LIBBY HOUSE

Portland, ME, 1858–60

While the Italianate style originated in Italy, it was filtered through England before arriving in America. The first Italianate house, Cronkhill, in Shropshire, was designed in 1802 by leading British architect John Nash (1752–1835). Cronkhill's Italian features found widespread favor in America by the 1850s. More akin to medieval Italian villas than to those of the Renaissance, Italianate houses often have a tower (or a cupola) and a low-angled roof with extended bracketed eaves. Victoria Mansion is more elaborate than the typical Italianate house. Built of brownstone from Portland, Connecticut, it has boldly carved window surrounds and Ionic porches.

Portland, like so many coastal harbors, was settled in the first decade of the large Puritan migration, the 1630s. First called Casco, later Falmouth, its economy was based on fishing and trading. In its history, three times it was destroyed: twice by American Indian attacks and once by the British Navy during the Revolution. Picking itself up yet again, renaming itself Portland, it began to prosper until the 1807 Embargo act and the War of 1812 depressed all communities of coastal New England. Finally in 1820, when Maine became a state separate from Massachusetts, Portland became its capital. This position lasted until 1832, when the state capital was moved to Augusta. Calamity visited the city once again when the July 4 celebration of 1866 resulted in a fire that devastated the commercial district, half the churches, and hundreds of homes. Like the mythological Phoenix, Portland rose again from the ashes, this time building in brick. As noted by Chicago, calamity breeds vigor: from then on Portland built a strong economy and a large number of fine Revival-style houses, many designed by accomplished architects drawn to a city ready for renewal.

Ruggles Sylvester Morse (1816–1893) was born and raised in Leeds, Maine. He went to New Orleans and became the proprietor of luxury hotels. His wealth established, he and his wife Olive Ring Merrill (1820–1903) decided to escape the summer heat, returning to Maine to build a sumptuous summer home in Portland. They contracted for architect Henry Austin of New Haven, Connecticut, to design, and erected (1858–60) what many consider the most elegant and richly detailed Italiante house in America.

The interiors and all the furnishings were commissioned of Gustave Herter of New York, one of his earliest design projects before he and his brother Christian established the firm of Herter Brothers in 1864, the leading exponent of what we refer to as American Renaissance design. Victoria Mansion is the only Herter commission that is sill intact. The richness of surfaces and furniture is almost without precedent in The United States at this time.

OPPOSITE *The hall contains an innovative central "flying" staircase leading to galleries on the second and third floors. Above the tall, narrow space is an ornamental stained-glass skylight that illuminates the central core of the house. The gasolier, hall chair, and bronzes on pedestals are all original to the house.*

RIGHT *The reception room is a catalog of the finest workmanship of its time, predating by a generation the finest mansions of Newport. The original furnishings, all dating to c.1860, include a sofa, chairs, and cabinet by Gustave Herter of New York, carpet by James Templeton & Co. of Glasgow, Scotland, and decorative painting on the walls and ceiling by Giuseppe Guidicini, an Italian émigré also based in New York City.*

TOP *The skylight's decorative glass includes reconstructions of the original allegorical stained glass roundels representing the four seasons, this one being "Summer," painted in 2001.*

MIDDLE *Among the original skylight roundels representing the four seasons, all enamel-painted on glass and dating to c.1859, this one of "Spring" is the sole survivor of the hurricane that destroyed the skylight in 1938. Remarkably, more than ninety percent of the contents of the house still remain from the Morse era, making the mansion a unique place to study the extraordinarily sophisticated lifestyle of America's elite on the eve of the Civil War.*

BOTTOM *The original stained-glass panels flanking the porch door at the back of the hall incorporate floral details, including lilies and this passionflower.*

OPPOSITE *The illumination from the skylight over the central hall could be supplemented with artificial light from the original two-tier gasolier suspended below it.*

Today, a veritable time-capsule, more then ninety percent of the contents are original. Many surfaces are covered with wall paintings by Italian immigrant Giuseppe Guidicini, who had begun his career as a theatrical scene painter. The rooms display uniformly elaborate features: marble mantles, plaster work ceilings, carved woodwork, and stained glass. Their harmonious balance is a testament to Herter's exceptional gifts as a designer. One has to visit Newport mansions built years later to appreciate Morse's foresight. An experienced hotel man, he was technologically advanced, installing central heating, gas lighting, hot and cold running water, and a servants call system.

The Morses had no children. When Ruggles died in 1893 his widow sold the house to Joseph Ralph Libby, the founder of a prominent Maine department store. Libby and family lived there until 1928, preserving it as built. Changes in the local economy and in fashions, however, left the viability of the house uncertain until one William H. Holmes saved it from possible demolition, establishing it as a museum in 1941, named in honor of Queen Victoria. In 1943 the Victoria Society of Maine Women assumed ownership. Now known as Victoria Mansion, this non-profit organization runs and operates the building as an historic house museum.

OPPOSITE *The parlor or drawing room was also designed and furnished by Herter, who drew heavily on French sources for this and other rooms. Here the room reflects the eighteenth-century revival style favored by Napoleon III's wife Empress Eugénie. Gustave Herter was trained in Stuttgart before emigrating to New York in 1848. He began his own firm in 1858 and the Morse home is his first documented commission for an entire house and the only one that survives intact today. After Gustave's brother Christian became a partner in 1864 the company was renamed Herter Brothers.*

RIGHT *The parlor or drawing room. The rosewood side table, inscribed "Morse" underneath the marble top, is signed by Gustave Herter. The painting by Luther Terry, Jacob's Dream, was acquired by Morse from the prominent James Robb collection in New Orleans while the mansion was under construction. Herter created the custom frame so it could hang in this location. Luther Terry,* Jacob's Dream, *1850–51, gift of Mrs. Ralph G. Libby, Sr.*

LEFT *Gustave Herter's European training and access to published continental design sources made him a leading cabinetmaker to the newly wealthy industrialists of America. This built-in carved oak sideboard, c.1860, one of three in the room, reflects avant-garde ideas about Renaissance design that were current in Europe at the time. The French porcelain and Sheffield silver-plate tray were Morse possessions.*

BELOW LEFT *Detail of the dining room marble mantel. The burgeoning wealth of America attracted the finest European craftsmen, including superb marble carvers from Italy. Their sure touch imparted a vigorous plasticity to the mansion's seven mantelpieces. When it came to culture at least, America's inventive industrialists turned out to be slavish imitators of the Old World.*

OPPOSITE *The advantage of retaining Herter's services is everywhere evident throughout the house. His knowledge of historic design and sensibility for appropriate form, color, and material were truly masterful. Public appreciation of his furniture is widespread, but one must come to Victoria Mansion to see the genius of his interior design, whereby all the elements of a room are meticulously coordinated to create a unified total ensemble. The dining room's chestnut paneling, oak furniture, and trompe-l'oeil grain-painted ceiling rise to an elegance only rarely achieved in mid-nineteenth-century American interiors. The Morses' porcelain, glassware, and silver are displayed on the original table.*

LEFT *The crest of the library armchair is carved with a shield set against Gothic tracery and inscribed "M" for the original owners, Ruggles Sylvester Morse and his wife Olive Ring Merrill Morse.*

RIGHT *The library departs from the other rooms in having natural walnut surfaces carved in the Gothic style, a style that was frequently used in the period for rooms devoted to reading and study. Again, the furniture is by Gustave Herter, who, according to the 1860 census, employed 100 craftsmen. The carpet dates to 1915.* Library table and side chairs gift of the Ralph Engelsman family in memory of Joan Chamberlain Engelsman.

STONEHURST
THE ROBERT TREAT PAINE HOUSE

Waltham, MA, 1866, 1886

Waltham was an early town of the Puritan migration (1634). Originally a part of Watertown, it was incorporated separately in 1738. Its location on the Charles River was its destiny; several dams created waterpower for early manufacturing, including textile mills and the first American assembly line for making watches—the American Waltham Watch Company.

Robert Treat Paine (1835–1910) was of an old Boston family (Thomas Paine was an ancestor and his great grandfather, of the same name, was a signer of the Declaration of Independence) who did well by himself, so he could do well for others. A lawyer and investor in railroads and mines, he married Lydia Lyman, only child of a wealthy shipping magnate who provided the newlyweds with a parcel of land adjacent to his own home in Waltham. In 1866 the Paines built a modest summer house in the French Second Empire style with mansard roof. Retired at the age of thirty-five, Paine devoted his energies to a number of social issues, becoming a prominent social reformer. He founded building and loan associations and organizations to teach crafts to the working class in Boston. He was one of the first to advocate that social problems could be best understood through scientific study.

The house is at one with its landscape, made more so by collaboration with landscape architect F. L. Olmstead. The old house was nearly hidden as a servants wing by Richardson's massive addition, anchored by towers like a Norman stone castle at hilltop. Olmstead's retaining walls hold back earthenware embankments.

Through his speeches and writings he promoted philanthropy and charitable giving as practical aids for social problems. He built affordable housing for working families, advocating a self-help philosophy: "Not alms, but a friend."

At home, with ten servants and seven children, the country house proved too small, so in 1883 the Paines undertook to enlarge it. While chairman of the building committee for the future Trinity Church in Boston (1872–77), Paine got to know its architect, Henry Hobson Richardson (1838–86) and, through him, landscape architect Frederick Law Olmsted (1822–1903). Both were the leading figures in their respective fields, and happened to be neighbors and friends in nearby Brookline, although their influence extended nationwide. Richrdson's career was launched by receiving the commission for Trinity Church, a masterpiece of ecclesiastical architecture for its time. So, when Paine asked him to work on a house addition—Richardson usually eschewed domestic projects in favor of large public buildings—he must have felt an endearing obligation, which he also extended to Olmsted. Olmsted likely appreciated a shared philosophy with Paine—both believed in the restorative power of the landscape as a balance against the debilitating forces of modern cities.

From 1883 to 1886, what was to become known as Stonehurst began as the old house was first moved to a high ridge with a sweeping view selected by Olmsted. Inspired by a "Glacier Rock," which dominated the view, the collaborators worked out plans for house and grounds that utilized natural materials from the site, seamlessly integrating them within the setting. The result was organic, a home that grew out of its site and was visually comfortable in it. Olmsted and Richardson were introducing to America a principal of building and landscape architecture that would influence their respective fields for generations—that one starts by discovering the genius of the natural site and then builds upon that figurative rock. Stonehurst is the only surviving house expressing their collaboration.

Richardson constructed the first story of massive glacial rocks from the property, inserting his trademark wide Romanesque stone arch at the entryway. The second floor is in shingles, a material Richardson and others used to appealing affect, leading to many houses in this new Shingle Style. A high stone tower artfully conceals the conjunction of the old house and the new addition. The interior is a high point in Richardson's career (it was also his last, for he died while the house was being finished). The great hall and summer parlor are one multi-functional space with intimate inglenooks and divider screens, all designed for the free flow of light and air. To create such a broad space Richardson suspended the coffered ceiling from tie rods hung from a truss. The public areas display his affection for the English Arts and Crafts Movement; much is richly carved and paneled in natural woodwork;

LEFT *In this private space allusions to humanistic sources of the architect's inspiration are found in the fireplace surround, a Renaissance-decorated mantle beam supported by caryatids familiar to that time.*

ABOVE *Naturalism of design finds its ultimate expression in a bay window corbel—a cat head, reminiscent of the same motif, called catheads, on sailing ships.*

ABOVE *The summer parlor is configured for that season; large, lighter in hue, larger in glass, a fireplace for focus, not fire. The inglenook screening, of Japanese inspiration, defines the space without excluding light and air.*

OPPOSITE *The private dining room. The rooms are carefully modulated compositions of natural surfaces, textures, and earth colors bathed in ample natural light.*

FOLLOWING PAGES *The living hall fireplace and curved window seat. The open-plan, multiple function space of today's fashion was long anticipated by Richardson's "living hall" just as he had appreciated the medieval great halls of Europe. The need of a house to serve two opposed functions—family privacy yet public space—is behind the oscillating space-sizing of styles of architecture, modulated, of course, by the type of heating systems which can efficiently create comfort.*

there are several magnificent marble and tile fireplaces. The stairway has such a mass that it appears to be flowing in its space.

Richardson's designing technique is explained by his own comment: "The architect acts on his building, but his building reacts on him—helps to build itself. His work is plastic work, and, like the sculptor's, cannot be finished in a drawing."

His use of horizontal banks of windows, natural wood surfaces, earthly color tones and open plan were important influences on Frank Lloyd Wright.

Olmsted, as well, utilized glacial boulders for the curved terrace, of which he wrote "I have never done any of the kind that I liked as much." Throughout the large landscape he chose to utilize native plants and trees, the result is a high compliment to a landscape designer, that his work, although extensively contrived, appears entirely natural.

Stonehurst, the Robert Treat Paine Estate, and the Storer Conservation Lands are owned and operated by the City of Waltham, Massachusetts. The non-profit Robert Treat Paine Historical Trust works in partnership with the city to preserve this National Historic Landmark and maintain it as an educational resource for a broad audience.

LEFT *A tower bedroom.*

ABOVE *The front bedroom window is more explicitly derivative than other features of the house. Georgian-like, it recalls the ancestral homes of the Paine family.*

ISAAC BELL JR. HOUSE

Newport, RI, 1881–83

From the 1630s Rhode Island drew settlers seeking a refuge for differing beliefs, including a group of Puritan dissenters who founded Newport in that decade. Their belief in tolerance continued for generations as immigrants of many faiths came here, including Jews, Quakers, and Baptists. Tolerance, opportunity, and ready access to the sea made Newport the principal port and colonial capital of Rhode Island in the eighteenth century up until the Revolution. Its sense of acceptance extended to other activities in the pursuit of wealth. Piracy was broadly practiced; only occasionally suppressed by authorities. Newport was also the center of the slave trade in New England, the basis of many fortunes. Needless to say when the Revolution began, Newporters were ready to throw off British authority. British occupation of the town stunted its population, trade, and prominence; the capital was moved to Providence and Newport never recovered its preeminence as a port. After the war two hundred abandoned buildings were torn down, many of them the cream of Georgian architecture.

Newport languished for decades until a new opportunity descended in the form of tourists, wealthy southern planters seeking summertime escape from the oppressive heat of home. From the 1840s on, Newport became an increasingly desirable

Colonial Revival homes tend to reflect inspiration from the colonial or more explicit copying of it. The Bell House double gable is an inspiration from early New England houses as is the use of shingle siding. The wraparound porch is a response to its immediate purpose, a coastal summer home.

189

LEFT *The entry inglenook or chimney corner explicitly references colonial features, a settle bench and a large Georgian-style fireplace with Delftware tiles.*

OPPOSITE *The entryway holds additional colonial inspirations. Besides the settle bench there is molded board paneling, a two-part door (more Dutch than New England) and a reference to colonial crewel embroidery. The emphasis on mellow wood rather than painted surfaces reflects the then current idea of what the earliest New England interiors were like.*

FOLLOWING PAGES *The dining room. Despite exterior features derived from the colonial, interior spaces come out of the Aesthetic Movement, each space interpreted differently.*

ABOVVE *Fireplace detail from the entryway.*

RIGHT *The entrance hall. The highly stylized carving was salvaged from nineteenth-century Breton folk furniture—a bed box and armoires—the chestnut bed box opening reveals the stairway. Such eclecticism, the mixing of motifs, was especially characteristic of late-nineteenth houses such that it is difficult to characterize some as predominantly of one style.*

summer resort town for the rich: first the planters, then those who had made fortunes in the China trade, and, finally, in the 1880s and 1890s, the wealthiest of industrial barons. They built what they called "summer cottages," a false modesty for extravagant mansions in many styles, some rivaling the chateaux of France.

One of those southern planters was Isaac Bell, a successful cotton broker and investor, who commissioned the New York firm of McKim, Mead & White in 1881 to build a proper upper class summer home on fashionable Bellevue Avenue where he and his family could reciprocate the elegant balls and dinner parties which characterized the social scene. The design was the work of all of the partners in the firm. It proved innovative (perhaps too innovative for some among Bell's conservative social class) because it combined elements of style from disparate sources: Continental, English Arts and Crafts, American colonial, and even Japanese.

Charles McKim and Stanford White had previously worked under H. H. Richardson who had pioneered the Shingle Style in the nearby Watts Sherman House (and would employ it again in 1883 at Stonehurst, p. 176), but when the firm took on the Bell House they evolved the style by simplifying trim and surfaces, emphasizing Colonial Revival features. It proved to be a turning point in the careers of the firm's principals and a milestone in American architecture. It was one of the first of the new Shingle Style houses, a combination of the colonial and Queen Anne clad in shingles, so natural to, and compatible with, a seaside environment. Being a summer house, it was refreshingly open and informal in plan, with extensive verandahs to take in views and healthy fresh air. Its form spread out horizontally in keeping with the open landscape, rather than imposed upon it. It was a perfect match of design to place and purpose. Countless houses would follow (and still follow today) this formula.

As with so many other "white elephants," as Newport visitor Henry James called them, the dark times of the twentieth century (two World Wars, the advent of federal income tax, and The Great Depression) put an end to most of the wealth expended on such extravagant living. The Bell House was sold for apartments and then a nursing home before being rescued by the Preservation Society of Newport County in 1994 and extensively restored. The wealth of the few has in three short generations become the pat-

HILL-STEAD
THE ALFRED POPE HOUSE

Farmington, CT, 1896

Where other communities go through long cycles of prosperity and decline, Farmington from its start in the 1630s has been remarkably prosperous, first from agriculture, then international trade (Farmington East India Company, for example), followed by mills and manufacturing. Today it is "Preservation's Valley," attracting homeowners and tourists to its scores of period houses. One such family developed its largest estate, Hill-Stead.

Hill-Stead is not the usual product of local merchant made good, rather, it is a return to nostalgia. Alfred A. Pope (1842–1913) grew up in New England but followed industrial opportunity to Cleveland, Ohio, where at age thirty-seven he rose to be president of Cleveland Malleable Iron Company. In his fifties, he and his wife yearned to return to the place of family and friends, New England. Meanwhile his daughter and only child, Theodate (1867–1946), had gone to Miss Porter's school in Farmington (1886–8). No Victorian wallflower, she was independent, energetic, and full of conviction. A Grand Tour of Europe with her parents helped nourish in her a love for early English vernacular homes and landscapes. She decided to acquire an early house in Farmington

Hill-Stead is a large country house incorporating many function-specific spaces. The challenge for Theodate Pope was to encapsulate so many rooms without the Colonial-style structure appearing to be an awkward agglomeration of blocks. This she tried to do by employing uniform materials. A dominating Mount Vernon–style portico with matching wings for family and guests could hide the long wing of servant and service rooms, followed by carriage barn and stables behind the main facade.

ABOVE *The entry hall was inspired by late-Georgian New England staircase hallways. The expansiveness created by large doorways is possible with post-colonial whole-house heating systems, not room-by-room fireplace heat, which closed up early houses. Beyond are two libraries, another post-colonial phenomena.*

RIGHT *Looking to the right from the entry hall is the drawing room, convenient to the dining room (through the door at left) for withdrawing from dinner, leaving the table to the men. Over the mantle is Claude Monet's 1888* View of Cap d'Antibes.

ABOVE *The second library is more a sitting room than a book depository, furnished, like much of the house, with American antiques, appropriate pieces for a Colonial Revival home. James McNeill Whistler, a friend of Alfred Pope, painted* The Blue Wave, Biarritz *in 1862. International flourishes can be seen on the mantle, including Chinese and Grecian pottery and French sculpture.*

OPPOSITE *Mantle detail.*

to create a farm for herself she called The O'Roukery. Its planning and restoration convinced her that architecture was her *métier*. She proposed to her parents that their return to New England should be her means to a masterwork building project. They agreed and the firm of McKim, Mead & White was retained to carry out her plans for her parents' country farm next to her own. It was, in effect, her apprenticeship in architecture. In time she became a licensed architect with several commissions, including three school campuses to her credit, the most ambitious being nearby Avon Old Farms School, which she created, funded, and led for years.

Her parent's home was created during 1896–1901 as a grand scale white clapboard Colonial Revival house with a complex of farm outbuildings set within a naturalistically landscaped 250 acres. Her landscape work is impressive, and takes advantage of existing topographical features and distant vistas. At great expense, the thin rocky New England hillside was planted with mature trees, stone walls, sunken and wild gardens, a large greenhouse, a pond, a six-hole golf ground, and kitchen and cutting garden. The lessons she had learned in England resulted in a new estate appearing as if it had been there for generations.

ABOVE *The "Ell" room is one of those extra rooms Pope included, its function to provide an intimate extension of a larger living room meant for small social gatherings. Its prominent exhibition of Monet's arresting* Grain Stacks in Bright Sunlight, *1890, brings as much inspired light to the room as the windows.*

RIGHT *The drawing room as viewed from the entry hall, features Edouard Manet's* Toreadors *(1863) and* The Guitar Player *(1866) as well as a 1901 Steinway piano necessary for musicals.*

FOLLOWING PAGES
Alfred Pope's discerning interest in the fine arts led to informed purchases, in evidence here and throughout the house.

The dining room, like many of the public rooms, is large yet not of proportionally high ceilings. Pope's choice of lower ceilings, some rooms with boxed "summer" beams, may reflect her desire to convey intimacy over grandeur, comfort over pomp. Edgar Degas's Jockeys, *1886, is over the mantle.*

The green guest room would pass for a Federal period bedroom but for the convenience of its own bathroom, furniture for lounging, writing, and tea, all conveniences for guests, a little home within a house. Expressive of that intimacy is Mary Cassatt's captivating Sara Handing the Toy to the Baby, *c.1901.*

Even after her parents moved there in 1901, more additions and changes took place, some by Theodate's hand, others by McKim, Mead & White. For Theodate, it was a work of art in progress, continuing after her father's death in 1913. Her marriage to diplomat John Wallace Riddle in 1916 opened opportunities for more travel and learning, which informed her other building projects. When she died in 1946 she provided for Hill-Stead to become a museum, which it has remained, mostly unchanged architecturally, to this day.

The Sunken Garden, designed by Beatrix Farrand and named for a natural depression in the landscape, is framed by a dry-laid stone wall within which are 36 flower beds with 90 plant varieties chosen so some are in bloom all season. In the center the summer house provides a restful shaded panorama of the entire garden.

ROSECLIFF

Newport, RI, 1898–1902

There is a consistent pattern to the creation of great houses in America. In almost all cases they derive from the results of resources, opportunity, entrepreneurial acumen, and a social system built on demonstrating achievement in order to establish prestige. The founder of a family dynasty needs to do this to be accepted in a social class to confirm his personal achievement, to help insure its perpetuation, and to bequeath it to his heirs. This is quite different from the British class system, which in principle is still based on hereditary title, although earned wealth, military achievement, and advantageous marriage have always been vehicles for entry into the upper class.

So when Irish immigrant James G. Fair, and partners, struck it rich with the Nevada Comstock Lode silver mine, he could dream of a wonderful new life. But it was his Virginia City–born daughter Theresa who realized the dream in a singular American way. With her inheritance and marriage to Herman Oelricks, American agent of the Norddeutscher Lloyd steamship line, she bought a prime parcel of land in the middle of Newport's Gold Coast and set out to build a palace worthy of a leading lady in society. In 1899 she hired the best architects, McKim, Mead & White, to design a summer "cottage" for entertaining on a grand scale and thereby became one of the leading hostesses of Newport. Stanford White

The east facade entrance to Rosecliff is a grand statement of French adaptation of Renaissance design principles. Rosecliff demonstrates that the major facade can be equally imposing whether or not the central block advances, as with most structures, or flanking wings advance, as here.

PRECEDING PAGES *The drama of stair hall and vestibule was created by Stanford White through juxtaposition of a romantic curvilinear French stairway and a classical rectilinear Italian vestibule—an artful interplay of basic emotional dispositions that have animated European and American art for centuries.*

ABOVE *The ballroom is a carefully orchestrated composition of visual animation, no surface at rest, all working together to dazzle the eye, drawing attention from one feature to the next. Even the parquet floor plays its part.*

OPPOSITE *The ballroom alcove was designed to contain an Aeolian pipe organ. Today it holds a Steinway.*

The Louis XVI–style dining room.

presented her with Rosecliff, an adaptation of the King Louis XIV's Grand Trianon near Versailles. White's version was a bit smaller in plan but two stories high with the same arched windows and paired Ionic pilasters. She no doubt asked for the romantic hearth-shaped double stairway (thereafter know as "the sweetheart staircase") and the biggest ball room in Newport (40-by-80 feet). Instead of pale rose terracotta facing, White used white in keeping with Mrs Oelrich's mania for cleanliness (beds changed each day regardless if slept in). Her most famous party was the "Bal blanc" of August 19, 1904, in celebration of the Astor Cup Races; everything was white and silver, her personal colors.

The house remained in the Oelrichs family until 1941 when contents were auctioned and the property sold, and then sold again several times, until a Mr. Monroe and his wife, a sugar magnate escaping New Orleans summers, bought it with enough means to continue the party style of the Newport heydays. They gave Rosecliff in 1971, with contents, to the Preservation Society of Newport County, which has opened it to the public. It may be familiar to moviegoers from the film *The Great Gatsby*, in which it appeared.

218

THE MOUNT

EDITH WHARTON'S ESTATE AND GARDENS

Lenox, MA, 1901–02

Lenox was a prosperous town in pastoral Berkshire County in western Massachusetts by the early nineteenth century. Its destiny, like other well-situated communities in New England and elsewhere, arose from three conditions: hot steamy cities wherein newly wealthy industrialist families perspired in thick clothes; delightfully appealing cool seaside and mountain landscapes; and new railroad and steamship lines spreading out through the countryside and along seashores and rivers ready to put the two together. The very families who owned those lines were the first to head for the hills and shores in their Pullman coaches; to the Catskill Mountains, the Adirondacks, the Berkshires, the White Mountains, Newport, the North Shore, and Maine. Newport and the Berkshires especially became the summer homes of New York City's elite; the big decision for socially conscious families was which was more preferable.

Great houses are as much about personalities as architecture. Edith Wharton (1862–1937) was just such a person. Born Edith Newbold Jones to wealthy parents in New York City, in her early years she and her family spent years in Paris, Rome, and Florence, then summering in Newport, where she met her future husband, Edward Robbins Wharton. In 1885 they married, dividing their

The Mount was largely inspired by the Brownlow family's Belton House of 1685–88 in Lincolnshire, England. With both houses, a pedimented central pavilion is flanked by projecting wings. The Mount, however, is raised on high ground above stoned terrace, the better to receive a commanding view of the landscape.

time between New York, Newport, and Europe. Edith was a serious student of life and culture, and from a young age was determined to be a writer, both of the follies of her class (*The Age of Innocence* won a Pulitzer Prize; and she was later awarded an honorary doctorate from Yale) and of great houses, their decoration, and gardens. In collaboration with designer Ogden Codman Jr., she published in 1897 *The Decoration of Houses*, a popular and influential book on architecture and interior design.

Shortly thereafter she undertook to practice what she preached by buying land at Lenox in the Berkshire Hills of western Massachusetts and designing and building a remarkable house, The Mount, taking up residence there in 1902. Tired of the frivolity of Newport life, The Mount was to prove the value of her taste, secure her privacy, and help an ailing marriage. There she wrote and published *The House of Mirth, Italian Backgrounds, and Italian Villas and their Gardens*, assuring her success in two literary genres. Alas, the marriage failed. They sold The Mount in 1911 and she moved to France for the remainder of her life, divorcing her husband two years later.

The Mount remained a private home for years, then a girls school; when a developer aspired to redo the property this prompted a preservation effort, which resulted in its purchase in 1980 by the Edith Wharton Restoration, Inc., a not-for-profit organization established to restore and preserve The Mount as a tribute to its creator.

The Mount reflects Wharton's strong preference for classical architecture; its exterior was inspired by Belton House, an especially pleasing English Palladian country house of 1684–86. On the inside she added her choice of classical Italian and French features plus a Georgian Revival gatehouse and stable, and several gardens, including an Italian walled garden. It is a whopping 16,850 square feet on four floors plus a cupola with forty-two principal rooms.

While the house carried out her prescription for a proper residence in accordance with *The Decoration of Houses*, she worked with seasoned professionals to carryout her vision: Francis L.V. Hoppin (of Hoppin & Koen, and formally an apprentice with McKim, Mead & White), architect, provided the drawings for the house, outbuildings, gate, and gardens. Ogden Codman Jr., co-author of *The Decoration of Houses*, helped design the interiors. Wharton's niece, Beatrix Jones Farrand, a landscape designer, assisted with the kitchen garden and the drive.

Her close friend Henry James, an astute observer of social scenes, once remarked "No one fully knows our Edith who hasn't seen her in the act of creating a habitation for herself." The Mount proved to be just such an autobiographical house, expressive of her knowledge, taste, principles, and sense of design. As she has written: "The Mount was my first real home … its blessed influence still lives in me."

The dining room, like the drawing room, is
architecturally Wharton's design, the furnishings
and contemporary paintings are of recent execution.
The dining room fireplace is framed by imported
marble; the carved trophy panel of a duck (and the
inset fruit still-life painting above) are emblems of
the room's function.

FOLLOWING PAGES Seen from above, the Italian
garden takes on a different appearance than from
below. Organized like rooms, its appeal is analogous to
that of fine architecture. Close up, the individuality of
flowers and colors appeal to another side of our natural
aesthetics. The gardens are recreated in the form
originally planned by Wharton. This one, in its
rectilinear design and stone columned pergola, follows
closely early Italian gardens she wrote extensively
about in Italian Villas and their Gardens.

231

BEAUPORT
THE SLEEPER-McCANN HOUSE
Gloucester, MA, 1907–34

Gloucester claims to be the first settlement of Massachusetts Bay Colony since the Dorchester Company expedition arrived at Cape Ann in 1623, before Salem (1626) or Boston (1630). The land was not so fertile but a plenitude of forest did provide the raw materials for logging, in a century before Gloucestermen discovered their future fortune in Grand Banks fishing. That distant location was, however, dependent upon the invention of a sail boat of superior speed and seaworthiness; the Gloucester schooner was born in 1713, the first of a line of world class sailing vessels to come out of the ports of New England. By the Civil War, Gloucester was one of the busiest fishing ports in the world. Within a generation this picturesque port also attracted visitors. By 1900 an assorted group of summer residents, many with creative arts interests, were building stylish cottages, not in the extravagant Newport style, but of more human scale. To serve them and be served by their connections to others, Henry David Sleeper (1878–1934) built Beauport.

Henry Davis Sleeper (1878–1934) was born to a successful real estate family in Boston. Although somewhat sickly as a child and home schooled, he went on forays with his mother for antiques. He showed an aptitude for design, once creating an elaborate model of a Japanese garden on the family billiard table in their Marblehead summer home. Years later he was introduced by A. Piatt Andrews Jr. to Eastern Point, Gloucester, where Andrews had

This garden facade is more akin to late-nineteenth-century Gothic than its post-medieval forbears of two centuries before.

235

Henry David Sleeper had initially been inspired by
a visit in 1907 to Emily and Elise Tyson's inspired
restoration of Hamilton House (p. 66) and creation of
a garden cottage which incorporated paneling from an
early house. Primarily an interior designer inspired by
American colonial interiors and antiques, Sleeper's ever-
expanding house exterior took on an eclectic appearance,
its features colonial-related but uniquely arranged.
Beauport's exterior is a delightful mélange of creative
allusions to our extended period past.

A special delight of Sleeper's aesthetic sense was how he harmoniously arranged and illuminated historic objects of a particular color range—in the case of the items on the page opposite, amber in all its shades.

FOLLOWING PAGES
Living room.

Sleeper's gift for combining disparate objects with compatible color themes is especially noticeable here in the Octagon Room; objects from France, China, and America share yellow gilt and maple with reds and pinks, highlighted against a deep blue background.

designed and built a house for himself. In 1906, inspired by Andrews—the two bachelors became life-long friends—Sleeper did the same. Their congenial neighbors formed a social, artistic and intellectual colony called Dabsville, a source of inspiration and support for Sleeper who embarked on a career of interior designing and furnishing homes. He hired Norwegian-born Halfdan M. Hanson (1884–1952), an aspiring architect, to help him create Beauport, Hanson's first—and longest lasting—large project.

What they created over a twenty-five-year period was a fantasy house built over the rocks of Gloucester harbor with curious towers and dormers sheltering a labyrinth of rooms decorated and furnished with Sleeper's singular taste for literary and historical themes and furnishings, every space enlivened with tastefully acquired and arranged antique furniture, folk art, and ceramics. It was first of all a showcase for his designer skills, but also a delightful setting for summer parties with friends and clients and a personal refuge.

Creativity breeds curiosity; and Beauport was featured in many magazine articles, helping to define in the public conscience a different way of using the past. From 1906 to 1934 forty rooms evolved to display Sleeper's particular talents for juxtaposing rescued architectural elements with artfully arranged combinations of colors and collectables.

After Sleeper's death in 1934, Beauport remained untouched when it was sold to Mr. and Mrs. Charles E. F. McCann who, so taken with its personal integrity, used it with little change as their summer home. On their death, their children acceded to their par–ents' wishes to have Beauport preserved by giving it to SPNEA (The Society for the Preservation of New England Antiquities, now Historic New England). Of the thirty-five sites Historic New England now maintains, this is the one that draws the greatest visitation. It would seem that history with a personal touch best reaches out to the curiosity of our time.

LEFT *The library combines elements of several periods: arched Gothic, elliptical Federal, and book-cabinet Chippendale.*

OPPOSITE *The Mariner's Room displays another of Sleeper's creative visions. By stripping all original paint, the room emphasizes the sculptural qualities of eighteenth-century New England interior features, integrated by a common surface regardless of where from assembled. The grand federal doorway, originally from a house in Newport, R.I., is one of many architectural salvages Sleeper creatively uses throughout Beauport. The room is dedicated to retired Gloucester ship captains. Displayed on the table are nautical and Masonic tools, among which are a scrimshaw busk and* Kabbala.

FOLLOWING PAGES *Created in 1923 out of a two-story space, the China Trade Room is luxuriously covered with a hand-painted set of Chinese wallpaper originally owned by Robert Morris of Revolution fame in Philadelphia. Sleeper furnished the room with Chinese pieces, the McCann's substituted Chinese Chippendale and other objects in the Chinese style.*

Sleeper's success at integrating the unexpected by using color themes, in evidence throughout the house, has continued to be inspirational in American decoration.

LEFT *A ship model displayed on a Chinese funerary table (not shown) is said to be a replica of a China Trade vessel that has given its name to the Golden Step Room. It is the only white-walled room in the house and, bathed in tranquil cool light on accents of green hues, the room evokes a mood harmony. It is one of five dining rooms, replacing in 1920–21 the original west loggia.*

ABOVE *A cabinet in the Golden Step Room displays gold spoons and green majolica.*

LEFT *The Strawberry Hill Room was named for and inspired by the English home of antiquarian and novelist Horace Walpole, credited as the first Gothic Revival structure (begun in 1747). As here, Sleeper favored tiger maple, which was incorporated throughout the house. A casement window overlooks the Gloucester Harbor, the inspiration for the house's name.*

BELOW LEFT *The Red Indian Room, added in 1921, was named after two wooden Indian figures displayed in the enclosed porch. Making use of every space—even the attic—Sleeper configured tester beds to fit under the roofline. When the McCanns bought the house, they made this their master bedroom with its spectacular views of the harbor.*

OPPOSITE *The awkward geometry of this under-roof room is relieved by large-scale scenic wallpaper, its trees and flowered plants overreaching just as in nature.*

A. EVERETT AUSTIN HOUSE

Hartford, CT, 1930–40

Hartford was initially an outpost of the Dutch claim to the Connecticut River Valley until a flood of English immigrants put short shift to that (one Dutch house escapes recognition in nearby Wethersfield). As the state capital and a center for manufacturing during the nineteenth century, Hartford had the size and wealth to advance a cultural agenda, one part of which was the founding of the Wadsworth Atheneum. Despite important collections of American paintings, early New England furniture, and the J. Pierpont Morgan collection of European decorative arts, the museum was conservative in outlook and regional in interest. But, by the 1920s, it was about to have a generational change thrust upon it.

A. Everett "Chick" Austin Jr. (1900–1957) was a dynamo of creativity whose forays into art history, contemporary art, teaching, painting, acting, theater design, cooking, and exuberant living, leave one breathless. Born of a well-to-do family in Brookline,

Not far from Venice, Italy, the Austins discovered Villa Ferretti at Dolo. They were so taken with architect Vincenzo Scamozzi's 1596 stuccoed brick structure that they were resolved to copy in New England's preferred material, wood. With only small changes they succeeded in replicating the front facade, one of the few faithful copies of an Italian Renaissance building in America.

FOLLOWING PAGES *Artfully mixing period architectural elements and furnishings from France and Italy the Austins created a suite of harmoniously integrated Continental-style rooms, comfortable for themselves while exciting for others. The Rococo doors invite entry between living and music rooms.*

ABOVE *What in other houses would be a sideboard niche, in this smaller room contains a carved and gilt Bavarian Nymphenburg console table, its 1740s Rococo agitation reflected in surrounding patterns.*

RIGHT *The living room's eighteenth-century French-painted stone mantelpiece sets the frame of reference for a French salon.*

FOLLOWING PAGES
The living room's painted Italian scenic panels (eighteenth-century Turin) expand the room's horizon and create its internal atmosphere. The use of plain carpeting is a concession to modern notions of comfort.

The dining room's architectural character derives from the carved Bavarian Rococo end wall, including a bed niche, or boiserie. The walls are covered in reproduced Italian silk Baroque pattern or brocatelle in the manner of the room's period.

OPPOSITE *Likely inspired by sweeping Federal stairways of their native New England, the Austins captured their drama in the front hall staircase, augmented by Austin's marbled decoration.*

RIGHT *A seventeenth-century (Antwerp) sculpture of Saint Luke, patron saint of artists, fittingly blesses the house created by multitalented Chick Austin. At the second floor stair landing one experiences a sudden transition from the Baroque to the Modern.*

Massachusetts, supported by a doting but over-bearing mother, young Austin received the invaluable education of the Grand Tour several times over, plus a stint at Harvard. His diminutive size and impish manner as a child earned him the life-long nickname of "Chick." Schooled haphazardly in Europe and at Harvard, he proved to be creatively self-directed, multi-lingual, and passionate about then-neglected Baroque art and championing Modern art and architecture before most New Englanders knew it existed. At age 26, this *enfant terrible d'avant garde* was advocated for by one admiring professor to the directorship of the oldest museum in the country, the Wadsworth Atheneum.

More platform than position, director Austin became the evangelist for the overlooked arts, propelling a staid museum into the national limelight with dramatic exhibitions of the new and different, coming up with surprising but important acquisitions of old master and contemporary art, and drawing to Hartford leading artists in several fields. He was, in truth, a charismatic culturalist. A devoted family man despite a broad sense of identity, he married Helen of the leading Hartford clan of Goodwins (her uncle was the Atheneum's president). It was a partnership of shared passion—for all his enthusiasms. On their honeymoon tour of Italy they chanced upon one of Scamozzi's Renaissance villas and adapted its principles to an otherwise theatrical home which they built in Hartford, a perfect platform for artful entertaining of a widening international circle of pioneering lights in the arts.

The house openly displayed Austin's contradictions and acumen. Set far back from a street otherwise lined with traditional mansions, it presented a facade that projected a personalized classicism, originally all white then given a rich gray body against stark white trim, including full-height Ionic pilasters. Inside, seeming contradictions prevailed: eighteenth-century Baroque public rooms on the first floor, Modern minimalist decor above. Two-stories high, 85-feet wide, but just one-room deep, the house cemented Hartford's titillation over its flamboyant impresario director who, they acknowledged, brought them international fame but whom they still fretted over for his disdain of budget limits and entrenched sensibilities. It is astonishing that Chick and his board managed to co-exist for as long as they did, to 1944. With the war effort putting constraints on funds and fun, Austin took a leave of absence in Hollywood, his kind of town, but when he returned to Hartford the trustees asked for his resignation. Acceding to their wishes, he did so, and found a promising new venue for himself as the first director of the John and Mable Ringling Museum of Art in Florida, the largest collection of Baroque art in America. Austin, like the Ringlings, made his mark in dramatic spectacle performance.

The house in Hartford remained his true home for the rest of his life, and after his death stood as a silent reminder of his achievements in Hartford. In 1985 Helen and their children, Sally and David, gave it and its contents to the Atheneum. In a sense Chick was welcomed back to the museum when it accepted his house as its own.

APPENDIX

House Museum Addresses and Contact Information

MACPHEADRIS-WARNER HOUSE *p. 36*

The Warner House Association
150 Daniel Street
Portmouth, NH 03802-0895

ISAAC ROYALL HOUSE *p. 44*

The Royall House Association
15 George Street
Medford, MA 02155
info@royallhouse.org

JEREMIAH LEE MANSION *p. 56*

Marblehead Historical Society
170 Washington Street
Marblehead, MA 01945

HAMILTON HOUSE *p. 66*

Historic New England
40 Vaughan's Lane
South Berwick, ME 06908

HARRISON GRAY OTIS HOUSE *p. 80*

Historic New England
141 Cambridge Street
Boston, MA 02114

GENERAL GEORGE COWLES HOUSE *p. 90*
Privately owned

GARDNER-PINGREE HOUSE *p. 102*

Peabody Essex Museum
128 Essex Street
Salem, MA 01970

GORE PLACE *p. 114*

The Christopher Gore House
Gore Place Society
52 Gore Street
Waltham, MA 02453

RUNDLET-MAY HOUSE *p. 126*

Historic New England
364 Middle Street
Portsmouth, NH 03801

BROOKSIDE *p. 140*

The Wilcox-Cutts House Orwell, VT
183 Route 22A
Orwell, VT 05760

JUSTIN S. MORRILL HOMESTEAD *p. 152*

Vermont Division for Historic Preservation
Route 32
Strafford, VT 05072

VICTORIA MANSION *p. 164*

The Morse-Libby House
109 Danforth Street
Portland, ME 04101

STONEHURST *p. 176*

The Robert Treat Paine House
100 Robert Treat Paine Drive
Waltham, MA 02452
info@stonehurstwaltham.org

ISAAC BELL JR. HOUSE *p. 188*

Preservation Society of Newport County
70 Perry Street
Newport, RI 02840
info@newportmansions.org

HILL-STEAD *p. 196*

The Alfred Pope House
The Hill-Stead Museum & Garden
35 Mountain Road
Farmington, CT 06032

ROSECLIFF *p. 212*

Preservation Society of Newport County
548 Bellevue Avenue
Newport, RI 02840
info@newportmansions.org

THE MOUNT *p. 222*

Edith Wharton's Estate and Gardens
Lenox MA Edith Wharton Restoration, Inc.
2 Plunkett Street
Lenox, MA 01240-0974

BEAUPORT *p. 234*

The Sleeper-McCann House
Historic New England
75 Eastern Point Boulevard
Gloucester, MA 01930

A. EVERETT AUSTIN HOUSE *p. 254*

Wadsworth Atheneum
130 Scarborough Street
Hartford, CT 06015

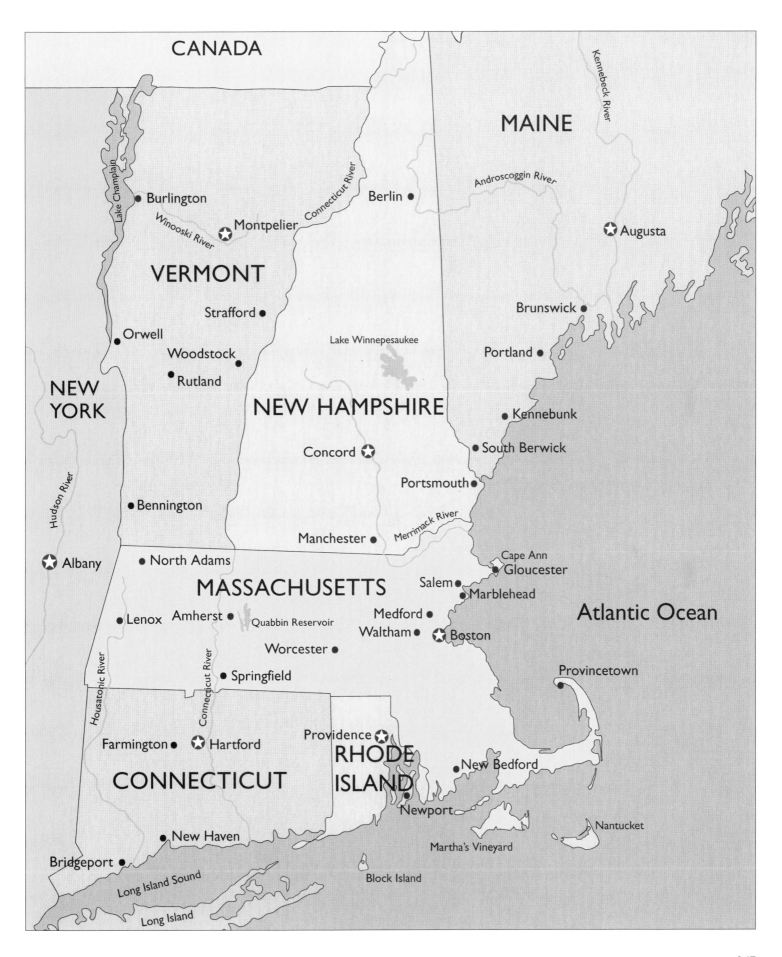

CANADA

MAINE

Kennebeck River

Androscoggin River

• Burlington

Berlin •

★ Augusta

Lake Champlain

Winooski River

Connecticut River

★ Montpelier

VERMONT

Strafford •

Brunswick •

Lake Winnepesaukee

• Orwell

Woodstock •

Portland •

NEW
YORK

• Rutland

NEW HAMPSHIRE

• Kennebunk

Hudson River

Concord ✪

• South Berwick

Portsmouth •

• Bennington

Merrimack River

Manchester •

Cape Ann

★ Albany

• North Adams

Gloucester

Salem •

Atlantic Ocean

MASSACHUSETTS

Marblehead

Housatonic River

• Lenox

Amherst •

Quabbin Reservoir

Medford •

Waltham •

★ Boston

Worcester •

Connecticut River

• Springfield

Provincetown
•

Farmington •

★ Hartford

Providence ✪

RHODE
ISLAND

• New Bedford

CONNECTICUT

Newport •

Nantucket

New Haven •

Martha's Vineyard

Bridgeport •

Long Island Sound

Block Island

Long Island

267

BIBLIOGRAHY

(An abbreviated list of useful sources on New England Architecture related to this book.)

Andrews, Wayne. Architecture in *New England: A Photographic History*. Brattleboro,VT.: S. Greene Press, 1973.

Beard, Frank A., and Bette A. Smith. *Maine's Historic Places*. Camden, ME.: Down East Books, 1982.

Garrett, Wendell. *Classic America: The Federal Style & Beyond*. New York: Rizzoli International Publications, 1992.

Garrett, Wendell. *American Colonial: Puritan Simplicity to Georgian Grace*. New York: Monacelli Press, 1995.

Garvin, James L. *A Building History of Northern New England*. Hanover and London: University Press of New England, 2001.

Hill-Stead: An Illustrated Museum Guide. Farmington, CT.: Hill-Stead Museum, 2003.

Howard, Hugh. *How Old Is This House? A Skeleton Key to Dating and Identifying Three Centuries of American Houses*. New York: Noonday Press, 1989.

Kimball, S. Fiske. *Domestic Architecture of the American Colonies and the Early Republic*. New York: Dover Publications, 1966 (reprint of 1922 edition).

Mallary, Peter T. *Houses of New England*. New York: Thames and Hudson, 1984.

Morrison, Hugh. *Early American Architecture from First Colonial Settlements to the National Period*. New York: Oxford University Press, 1952. Reprint, New York: Dover Publications, 1987.

Nylander, Jane C. and Diane L. Viera. *Windows on the Past, Four Centuries of New England Homes*. Society for the Preservation of New England Antiquities. New York: Bulfinch Press/ Little Brown and Company, 2000.

Roth, Leland M. and Bret Morgan. *Shingle Style, Innovation, and Tradition in American Architecture 1874 to 1982*. New York: Harry N. Abrams, Inc. Publishers, 1999.

Viera, Dianje. *Hamilton House: A Quintessential Colonial Revival Summer House in South Berwick, Maine*. Boston, MA: SPNEA (Society for the Preservation of New England Antiquities), [2000?].

Volk, Joyce Geary, ed. *The Warner House: A Rich and Colorful History*. Portmouth, NH.: The Warner House Association, 2006.

Ward, Gerald W. R. *The Gardner-Pingree House*. Salem, MA.: Essex Institute, 1976.

Waterman, Thomas Tileston. *The Dwellings of Colonial America*. Chapel Hill, NC.: University of North Carolina Press, 1950.

Whitehead, Russell F. and Frank Chouteau Brown, eds. *Architectural Treasures of America: Colonial Architecture of New England* [and related titles]. From materials originally published as The White Pine Series of Architectural Monographs. New York: The Early American Society, Inc., and Arno Press Inc., 1977.

Wilson, Richard Guy. *The Colonial Revival*. New York, Harry N. Abrams, Inc., Publishers, 2004.

ACKNOWLEDGMENTS

RODERIC H. BLACKBURN AND GEOFFREY GROSS

One of the nicest pleasures of doing a book is to reflect on the many people and organizations who came to our aid to provide essential expertise, knowledge, on-site assistance, and book production. We are pleased to mention each one and express our warm thanks for their many gifts of knowledge and time.

Ken Abramson accompanied Geoffrey on several trips and made many helpful photo suggestions. Lew Sussman always made room for us at his home and whipped up gourmet meals out of thin air. Logan Blackburn made all the difference by assisting on several locations as photographer's assistant. Alice Tobin-Gross provided much needed constructive criticism and very special retouching skills. Catherine Croner and Brandt Bolding, of the estate of photographer Ted Croner, made a generous gift of very much needed lighting equipment.

Also helpful with historical guidance and encouragement were: Jim McCallister, Earl Shettleworth, William B Finch, Linda Wilson, John Garvin, Richard Cheek, Sam White, Abbott Lowell Cummings, Richard and Jane Nylander, Thomas B. Johnson, Brandt Bolding, Barbara and David Kaufman, Paul and Lee Fopeano of Academy Street Inn, and Marla Johnson Truini.

Holly Holden of Holly Holden and Company, Ltd. ~ Classic Interior Design, A.S.I.D. Allied Member, who was most helpful with her expertise on one site.

The staff at Rizzoli we especially thank for their confidence in our ability to create the content of this book. These include, in particular, Charles Miers, David Morton, Douglas Curran, Maria Pia Gramglia, as well as Abigail Sturges and Gerrit Albertson of Sturges Design, all of whom assisted us with patience, indulgence, and limitless contributions to make this book a reality.

The staff members and owners of each of the sites have made possible the inclusion of many of New England's finest houses in this book. From first call to final exit they have shared in and inspired the photographic and textural vision expressed herein. We are so pleased to acknowledge our indebtedness to each for their contribution.

Macpheadris-Warner House: Joyce Geary Volk, Curator, Warner House Association.

Isaac Royall House: Thomas Lincoln, Executive Director and John J. Woods, President.

Jeremiah Lee Mansion: Judy Anderson, Curator.

Hamilton House: Peggy Wishart, Site Manager, Southern Maine Properties, Historic New England.

Harrison Gray Otis House: Susanna M. Crampton, Public Relations Officer, Historic New England.

Gardner-Pingree House: Dan L. Monroe, Executive Director & CEO, Peabody Essex Museum; Jay Finney, Chief Marketing Officer, Peabody Essex Museum; Dean Lahikainen, Carolyn Lynch, and Peter Lynch, Curator of American Decorative Art, Peabody Essex Museum; Kristen Weiss, Collections Manager; Marli Porth, Deputy to the Chief Operating Officer.

Gore Place, The Christopher Gore House: Lana Lewis, Collections Manager

Rundlet-May House: Elizabeth Farish, Maine and New Hampshire Regional Site Manager.

Brookside, The Wilcox-Cutts House: T. Tench Murray-Robertson, Sandy Sears, owners.

Justin S. Morrill Homestead: John P. Dumville, Historic Sites Operations Chief, Vermont Division for Historic Preservation.

Victoria Mansion, The Morse-Libby House: Thank you to the staff and Board of Trustees of Victoria Mansion, including Robert Wolterstorff, Director, Arlene Palmer Schwind, Curator, and Julia Kirby, Deputy Director, for their time and guidance with the photography shoot and input into the content and descriptions of Victoria Mansion.

Stonehurst, The Robert Treat Paine House: Ann Clifford, Director and Curator; photographs at the house made with permission from Stonehurst, The Robert Treat Paine Estate, an icon of American design owned by the City of Waltham, Massachusetts.

Isaac Bell Jr. House: Paul Miller, Curator, Preservation Society of Newport County.

Hill-Stead, The Alfred Pope House: Cindy Cormier, Director of Education and Curatorial Services; Melanie Anderson Bourbeau, Curatorial Assistant, Rebecca Guernsey.

Rosecliff: Paul Miller, Curator, Preservation Society of Newport County.

The Mount, Edith Wharton's Estate and Gardens: to the Staff at the Mount, including, in particular, Susan Wissler, Vice President, Molly McFall, Librarian, Toby Raymond, Marketing and Group Sales, Office Manager.

Beauport, The Sleeper-McCann House: Pilar Garro, Site Manager, Susanna Crampton, Elizabeth Farish, Peggy Wishart, Leah Walczak, and Jean Zove.

A. Everett Austin House: Gene Gaddis, Archivist and Curator of the Austin House, Wadsworth Atheneum.

And our own mutual appreciation: from Geoffrey: the warmest appreciation to Rod Blackburn as both mentor and writer. From Rod: to Geoffrey who spearheaded this project (as also with our prior book) both in idea and execution, whose special photographic gifts shall be with us forever.

INDEX

First published in the United States of America in 2008 by
RIZZOLI INTERNATIONAL PUBLICATIONS, INC.
300 Park Avenue South, New York, NY 10010
www.rizzoliusa.com

ISBN-10: 0-8478-3101-9
ISBN-13: 978-0-8478-3101-2
LCCN: 2007907649

Map of New England (p. 267) prepared by
Gerrit Albertson/Sturges Design.

This publication is made possible in part by grants from:
Furthermore, the publication program of the J. M. Kaplan Fund
The New York Foundation for the Arts

Designed by Abigail Sturges/Sturges Design.

Distributed to the U.S. trade by Random House, New York

Printed and bound in China

2008 2009 2010 2011 2012/ 10 9 8 7 6 5 4 3 2 1

To my wife, DeGuerre, who, fortunately for both of us, shares
in my passion for a visible heritage, especially architecture and
gardens.
—R.B.

To Alice, as always ... my little girl.
—G.G.